Best Practices for Teaching

READING

Other Corwin Press Books by Randi Stone

Best Practices for Teaching Social Studies: What Award-Winning Classroom Teachers Do, 2008

Best Practices for Teaching Writing: What Award-Winning Classroom Teachers Do, 2007

Best Practices for Teaching Mathematics: What Award-Winning Classroom Teachers Do, 2007

Best Practices for Teaching Science: What Award-Winning Classroom Teachers Do, 2007

Best Classroom Management Practices for Reaching All Learners: What Award-Winning Classroom Teachers Do, 2005

Best Teaching Practices for Reaching All Learners: What Award-Winning Classroom Teachers Do, 2004

What?! Another New Mandate? What Award-Winning Teachers Do When School Rules Change, 2002

Best Practices for High School Classrooms: What Award-Winning Secondary Teachers Do, 2001

Best Classroom Practices: What Award-Winning Elementary Teachers Do, 1999

New Ways to Teach Using Cable Television: A Step-by-Step Guide, 1997

Best Practices for Teaching

READING

What Award-Winning Classroom Teachers Do

RANDI STONE

CORWIN
PRESS
A SAGE Company

For information:

Corwin Press
A SAGE Company
2455 Teller Road
Thousand Oaks, California 91320
www.corwinpress.com

SAGE Ltd.
1 Oliver's Yard
55 City Road
London EC1Y 1SP
United Kingdom

SAGE India Pvt. Ltd.
B 1/I 1 Mohan Cooperative
   Industrial Area
Mathura Road, New Delhi 110 044
India

SAGE Asia-Pacific Pte. Ltd.
33 Pekin Street #02-01
Far East Square
Singapore 048763

Printed in the United States of America.

Library of Congress Cataloging-in-Publication Data

Best practices for teaching reading : what award-winning classroom teachers do/edited by Randi Stone.
      p. cm.
Includes bibliographical references and index.
ISBN 978-1-4129-2458-0 (cloth)
ISBN 978-1-4129-2459-7 (pbk.)
   1. Reading. 2. Effective teaching. I. Stone, Randi. II. Title.

LB1050.B468 2009
372.4—dc22   2008022902

This book is printed on acid-free paper.

08   09   10   11   12   10   9   8   7   6   5   4   3   2   1

Acquisitions Editor:	Carol Chambers Collins
Editorial Assistant:	Brett Ory
Production Editor:	Cassandra Margaret Seibel
Copy Editor:	Cheryl Rivard
Typesetter:	C&M Digitals (P) Ltd.
Proofreader:	Jennifer Gritt
Indexer:	Terri Corry
Cover Designer:	Scott Van Atta

Contents

Preface

Best Practices for Teaching Reading is the fifth book of a five-volume series: The collection also includes *Best Practices for Teaching Social Studies, Best Practices for Teaching Writing, Best Practices for Teaching Science,* and *Best Practices for Teaching Math.* This unique guide provides exemplary teaching practices from award-winning teachers who are willing to share their expertise. These are the teachers we read about in journals and magazines, the teachers who win grants, fellowships, and contests. Enjoy "poking your nose" into great classrooms!

Acknowledgments

Corwin Press acknowledges with gratitude the important contributions of the following manuscript reviewers:

Susan Bailey, Middle School Reading Specialist
Mequon Thiensville School District
Mequon, WI

Emma Barnes, Literacy Facilitator
Charlotte Mecklenburg Schools
Charlotte, NC

Jill E. Cole, Associate Professor of Education
Wesley College
Dover, DE

Connie Molony, Reading Intervention Teacher
    and Language Arts Specialist
Carl Ben Eilson Middle School, Fargo Public Schools
Fargo, ND

Shannan McNair, Associate Professor
Oakland University
Rochester, MI

Sara Spruce, Professor of Education
Olivet Nazarene University
Bourbonnais, IL

About the Author

Randi Stone is a graduate of Clark University, Boston University, and Salem State College. She completed her doctorate in education at the University of Massachusetts, Lowell. She is the author of eleven Corwin Press books, including her latest in a series: *Best Practices for Teaching Reading: What Award-Winning Classroom Teachers Do, Best Practices for Teaching Social Studies: What Award-Winning Classroom Teachers Do, Best Practices for Teaching Writing: What Award-Winning Classroom Teachers Do, Best Practices for Teaching Mathematics: What Award-Winning Classroom Teachers Do,* and *Best Practices for Teaching Science: What Award-Winning Classroom Teachers Do.* She lives with her teenage daughter, Blair, in Keene, New Hampshire.

About the Contributors

Stuart Albright, English and Creative Writing Teacher
C.E. Jordan High School
2704 Bexley Avenue
Durham, North Carolina 27707
School Telephone Number: (919) 943-6501 ext. 12754
E-mail: stuart.albright@dpsnc.net

Number of Years Teaching: 6
Awards: Milken Family Foundation National Educator Award, 2007
            Durham Public Schools Teacher of the Year, 2006
            Jordan High School Teacher of the Year, 2005

Caridad Alonso, First- Through Fifth-Grade Teacher
William C. Lewis Dual Language Elementary School
920 North Van Buren Street
Wilmington, Delaware 19806
School Telephone Number: (302) 651-2695
E-mail: Caridad.alonso@redclay.k12.us

Number of Years Teaching: 11
Awards: Delaware Teacher of the Year, 2007

Greg Andersen, Math Teacher
Rampart High School
8250 Lexington Drive
Colorado Springs, Colorado 80920

School Telephone Number: (719) 234-2000
E-mail: ganders@asd20.org

Number of Years Teaching: 21
Awards: Wal-Mart Colorado Teacher of the Year, 2006

Heather-Lee M. Baron, Reading Teacher and ESL Coordinator
Union City Middle-High School
105 Concord Street
Union City, Pennsylvania 16438
School Telephone Number: (814) 438-7673
E-mail: hlmbaron@aol.com

Number of Years Teaching: 6
Awards: Golden Apple Award presented by Edinboro University
            of Pennsylvania and JET-TV 24, 2008
            National ING Unsung Heroes Award, 2007

Donna Bradley, First-, Second-, and Third-Grade Teacher, ARI
(Alabama Reading Initiative) Reading Coach
Hollinger's Island Elementary School
2400 Hammock Road
Mobile, Alabama 36544
School Telephone Number: (251) 221-1376
E-mail: dbradley@mcpss.com

Number of Years Teaching: 16
Awards: Mobile Area Education Foundation Grant, 2007
            Martha Gaitlin Memorial Scholarship/Delta Kappa
              Gamma Society International, 2005
            Eleanor M. Johnson Reading Award,
              International Reading Association, 2001

Jacquylynn Brickman, Fourth-Grade Teacher
Elizabeth Hall International School
1601 Aldrich Avenue North
Minneapolis, Minnesota 55411
School Telephone Number: (612) 668-2660
E-mail: jbrickman@usfamily.net

Number of Years Teaching: 11
Award: Milken Educator Award, 2006

Susanne Burkhardt, Third-Grade Teacher
Simpsonville Elementary School
6725 Shelbyville Road
Simpsonville, Kentucky 40067
School Telephone Number: (502) 722-8855
E-mail: susanne.burkhardt@shelby.kyschools.us

Number of years teaching: 17
Awards: Kentucky Teacher of the Year, 2007
Kentucky Elementary Teacher of the Year, 2007
WHAS ExCEL Teacher, 2007

Susan Carter, First-Grade Teacher
Jackson Park Elementary School
7400 Balson Avenue
University City, Missouri 63130
School Telephone Number: (314) 290-4451
E-mail: scarter@u-city.k12.mo.us

Number of Years Teaching: 7
Award: Milken Educator Award, 2006

Michele Rzewski Copeland, Librarian
Potowmack Elementary School
46465 Esterbrook Circle
Sterling, Virginia 20165
School Telephone Number: (703) 444-7522
E-mail: mrzewski@loudoun.k12.va.us

Number of Years Teaching: 13
Awards: ING Unsung Heroes Award, 2007
NEA Innovation Award grant recipient, 2006

Maria I. Davis, Language Arts Teacher
John P. Parker Elementary School
3500 Lumford Place

Cincinnati, Ohio 45213
School Telephone Number: (513) 363-2900
E-mail: riaidavis1@hotmail.com

Number of Years Teaching: 15
Awards: Milken National Educator Award, 2007
            Scott Foresman National Teacher Award, 2000

Karen Morgan Delbridge, PhD, Instructional Facilitator
East High School
2800 East Pershing Boulevard
Cheyenne, Wyoming 82001
School Telephone Number: (307) 771-2663 ext. 21524
E-mail: ckdelbridge@aol.com and delbridgek@laramie1.k12.wy.us

Number of Years Teaching: 14
Awards: Richard W. Halle Award for Outstanding Middle Level
            Educator given by the National Council of Teachers
            of English (NCTE), 2006
            Hispanic Organization for Progress and Education
            (HOPE) Teacher of the Year, 2006
            Intellectual Freedom Award given by the National Council
            of Teachers of English (NCTE) and Support and
            Learning for the Teaching of English (SLATE), 2003

Anita Tortorici Dobbs, Seventh-Grade Math Teacher
Hewitt-Trussville Middle School
301 Parkway Drive
Trussville, Alabama 35173
School Telephone Number: (205) 228-3700
E-mail: anita.dobbs@trussvillecityschools.com

Awards: Wal-Mart State Teacher of the Year, 2006
            University of Alabama at Birmingham Outstanding
            Alumna, Elementary Education, 2002
            Presidential Award for Excellence in Mathematics and
            Science Teaching (PAEMST), 2000

Jill Dougherty, Reading Specialist
Springfield High School
49 West Leamy Avenue
Springfield, Pennsylvania 19064
School Telephone Number: (610) 772-6200
E-mail: doughjil@ssd.k12.pa.us

Number of Years Teaching: 9
Awards: Milken National Educator Award, 2007

Amy Edinger, Kindergarten, Special Education Teacher
James Fenimore Cooper Elementary School
1960 Greentree Road
Cherry Hill, New Jersey 08003
School Telephone Number: (856) 424-4554
E-mail: aedinger@chclc.org

Number of Years Teaching: 9
Award: New Jersey's No Child Left Behind American Star of
            Teaching Award, 2006

Jessica Galla, Reading Specialist
Lincoln High School
135 Old River Road
Lincoln, Rhode Island 02838
School Telephone Number: (401) 334-7500
E-mail: jlgalla@cox.net

Number of Years Teaching: 8
Awards: ING Unsung Heroes Award, 2004

Jenna Hallman, Second-Grade Teacher, Science Specialist
Calhoun Academy of the Arts
1520 East Calhoun Street
Anderson, South Carolina 29621
School Telephone Number: (864) 260-5090
E-mail: jennahallman@anderson5.net

Number of Years Teaching: 9
Awards: The Toyota Tapestry Grant, 2007
            District Five Teacher of the Year, 2007
            National Board Certification as an Early Childhood
            Generalist, 2003

Jessica Heidelberg, Title I Literacy Impact Teacher
Harcourt Elementary School
7535 Harcourt Road
Indianapolis, Indiana 46260
School Telephone Number: (317) 259-5458
E-mail: jheidelberg@msdwt.k12.in.us

Number of Years Teaching: 8
Awards: Milken Educator Award, 2006
            Washington Township Teacher of the Year, 2006

Linda Hennen, First-Grade Teacher
Mason-Dixon Elementary School
7041 Mason-Dixon Highway
Blacksville, West Virginia 26521
School Telephone Number: (304) 662-6113
E-mail: Linhennen@aol.com

Number of Years Teaching: 14
Awards: International Reading Association:
               Eleanor M. Johnson Award, 2005
            National Board Certified Teacher, 2001

Sharon S. Lancaster, First- and Second-Grade Teacher
Indian Hills Elementary School
313 Blane Drive
Hopkinsville, Kentucky 42240
School Telephone Number: (270) 887-7230
E-mail: Sharon.lancaster@christian.kyschools.us and
sharonlancaster@bellsouth.net

Number of Years Teaching: 15
Awards: Region I Finalist, Elementary Teacher of the Year, 2007
Ashland Inc. Teacher Achievement Award, 2003

Mikki Nuckols, Language Arts Teacher
Rocky Mountain Middle School
3443 N. Ammon Road
Idaho Falls, Idaho 83401
School Telephone Number: (208) 525-4403
E-mail: nuckolsm@d93.k12.id.us

Number of Years Teaching: 10
Awards: Milken Educator Award, 2007

Pamela Jo Roller, Second-Grade Teacher
Galveston Elementary School
404 South Maple Street
Galveston, Indiana 46932
School Telephone Number: (574) 699-6687
E-mail: rollerp@sesc.k12.in.us

Number of Years Teaching: 33
Awards: Japan Fulbright Memorial Fund Scholar, 2005
Disney Teacher Award, 2003

Jennifer Ruth, Literacy Specialist
Christie Elementary School
3801 Rainier Road
Plano, Texas 75023
School Telephone Number: (469) 752-0879
E-mail: jennifer.ruth@pisd.edu

Number of Years Teaching: 12
Awards: ING Unsung Heroes Award, 2007
Association of Texas Professional Educators Grant for
Teaching Excellence Finalist, 2007

Jill Saceman Ryerson, Seventh-Grade Language Arts/Reading Teacher
North Whitfield Middle School
3264 Cleveland Road
Dalton, Georgia 30721
School Telephone Number: (706) 259-3381
E-mail: jill_ryerson@whitfield.k12.ga.us

Number of Years Teaching: 15

Janet K. Vaine, Eighth-Grade Language Arts Teacher
Southside Middle School
2948 Knights Lane East
Jacksonville, Florida 32216
School Telephone Number: (904) 739-5238
E-mail: vainej@dreamsbeginhere.org

Number of Years Teaching: 20
Awards: Merit Pay Award, 2006–2007
             Creative Communications Poetry Contest, 2006–2007
             Creative Communications Essay Contest, 2006–2007

Summer Williams, Second-Grade Teacher
Cary Woods Elementary School
715 Sanders Street
Auburn, Alabama 36830
School Telephone Number: (334) 887-4940
E-mail: sbwilliams@auburnschools.org

Number of Years Teaching: 5
Awards: Recipient of Learning and Leadership
             Grant from NEA, 2006
             Intern with Nancie Atwell, 2006

Diane Woodford, Fifth-Grade Teacher
Covington Elementary School
2116 A Street
South Sioux City, Nebraska 68776
School Telephone Number: (402) 494-4238
E-mail: woodforddiane@hotmail.com

Number of Years Teaching: 31

Awards: Colonial Williamsburg Fellow, 2006

Morningside College (Sioux City, Iowa) Alumni Educator of the Year, 2005

Nebraska Teacher of the Year, 2004

Darrell Yater, Language Arts Teacher

White Oak Middle School

3130 Jessup Road

Cincinnati, Ohio 45239

School Telephone Number: (513) 741-4300

E-mail: yateda@nwlsd.org and djyater@aol.com

Number of Years Teaching: 13

Awards: Outstanding Regional Educator Award, Southwest Region, Ohio Middle School Association, 2008

Milken Educator Award, 2007

Hamilton County Educational Service Center Celebrate Excellence Award, 2007

To Susan Julian Gates, my inspiration

PART I

Reading in K–6 Classrooms

CHAPTER *1*

Reading From the First Day of School

Sharon S. Lancaster

Hopkinsville, Kentucky

H e stood in the computer center of my primary first- and second-grade classroom looking around with uncertainty and maybe even fear. His eyes darted to me while I talked with a parent during our open house. School would be starting in a week and this was the "Big Night" to come and meet your teacher and see your classroom. I smiled at him and there was a brief hint of a grin. As I walked over to meet my VIP (Very Important Pupil), he looked somewhat like a deer caught in the headlights. I could tell he really wasn't sure how he was supposed to respond. I bent down to where we could be eye-to-eye and asked his name. He responded rather timidly. I asked him what he liked to do and what he hoped to learn this year. I will never forget those great big brown eyes looking at me and his quiet voice saying, "I don't know how to read. I want to learn how to read."

I took his chin in my hand, looked directly into my eyes, and said, "I guarantee that on the first day of school you will be able to read something." He looked at me again with those enormous dark brown eyes, smiled, and said, "Promise?" "I promise," I assured him. With the solemn vow that passed between us, I knew I had to make certain that he would be able to read something that first day of school. I also knew that other parents were listening, and I could tell that they were skeptical about my promise.

The first day of school arrived and I welcomed all twenty-four of my children to the classroom. Some of them had attended the open house and we had met; others were seeing me for the first time. Six-year-olds have a way of remembering promises, and my little guy was no exception. He came in and wished me a good morning and found his seat. I could tell he was just waiting for me to teach him to read. We waded through all those first-day-of-school preliminaries and then the parents left. I told the class that I had made a promise to one of their classmates and that it was that they would be able to read something that very first day of school. I knew I had to hook them all and begin that slow process of teaching them not only to read but to love to read.

I found my new dry-erase markers in all eight colors, and I began to write on the board in red the word "red." I turned and asked the children, "What word do you think is up here?" My young man raised his hand and said tentatively, "Red?" "You are exactly right! Now give me a high five!" I smiled. I then proceeded to write each of the six color words in their respective color—blue, green, yellow, black, orange, brown— and then decided I would have to write the word "white" in black. I pulled this off by telling the children I was writing this color word in the opposite color hoping they remembered what *opposite* meant. I found out very quickly that they certainly did remember when many shouted, "White!!!" I looked over at my new student, who had a smile on his face that would light up a room. I knew I had piqued his interest.

It wasn't long before our curriculum specialist walked in to meet the children, and I told her that my children could already read. She played right along and asked me to prove it. The children were in their glory at that minute. The color words were still on the board and the children read them in unison. She turned to them and said, "I can't believe you all are already reading! I am so excited that we have such smart boys and girls at Indian Hills!" I told her about my promise. The children's confidence levels began to climb that very day. The color-word activity on the first day of school is the hook that catches the children and gives them confidence to tackle learning to read.

Another confidence builder is reading to the principal, guidance counselor, curriculum specialist, or secretary. These folks do a great job of encouraging and promoting reading. They listen, applaud, hug, and give a treat to the child. I want every child to be able to go to the office and read for someone before the year is over. This simple activity doesn't cost anything, but a little time and the rewards for my students come back tenfold.

I recently had a parent ask me what I had done to her child. My stomach did a flip, and I couldn't think of a thing that I had done because this child is a good student and very well behaved. I answered, "I don't know. What have I done to your child?" She answered, "All she wants to do is read! She didn't even want to pick up a book before she came to your class. Thank you so much and please keep up whatever it is you are doing! It is wonderful to see her enjoying reading and wanting to read."

The most rewarding part of teaching first grade is knowing that when my students leave my classroom, they can read, and they are taking a skill with them that no one can take from them.

Helpful Tips

- I echo read the story the first day it is introduced. I read one sentence at a time adding voice and following punctuation. I think that by modeling the correct form of oral reading, the children will follow suit.
- My students love to buddy read. I team a pair of students, one that is a good reader with one that may be struggling or just needs a little help.
- Peer tutoring is a lifesaver at times. I use peer tutoring in math also. Sometimes all it takes is a child explaining it to their classmate. I see rewards in this for both students. The one doing the tutoring is

reinforcing the skills they have learned, and the one struggling is benefiting from help by a peer.

- The students love making their own sight-word/vocabulary flash cards. This helps them because by writing the words, they are becoming familiar with the way the word is spelled and how each letter sounds. Our local print shops give us scrap card stock and they make perfect flash cards.

CHAPTER 2

Ten Steps to Great Readers

Susan Carter

University City, Missouri

When people visit my first-grade classroom during guided reading, they see a room filled with children absorbed in their own books. There are no literacy centers, no puzzles, no other activities but reading. Children are sitting with me at the reading table, others are in the classroom library, some are working on the computer, some are at their desk, and all are completely absorbed in the task at hand: reading. After about a half hour to an hour of observation, the visitor looks around and notices that the students are still reading and are still engaged in the task. The question they always ask is, "How do you make them read for so long?"

Some teachers say that their kids would never do it. They ask me where I got these kids. Others ask me what the reward is or what the punishment is for noncompliance. What do I do to them to make them read? There is no reward, no consequence. The truth is, I don't make them read. What I do is remove every possible, preventable obstacle to reading. I approach reading in first grade with one goal in mind: fearless, fluent readers. I anticipate distractions and remove them. I create an environment where they can read and give them the time and tools to become fearless, fluent readers. Every instructional or aesthetic decision I make in my classroom is enacted in light of that one lofty goal.

Learning to read and then being able to read anything is intrinsically rewarding. They don't come into the classroom reading independently for extended times. What has to happen in order for this to work? How do I teach them to love to read? There is no other incentive: reading is its own reward. It feels good to be a successful reader. But there has to be a trick, right? Of course there is. Actually, there are ten.

Ten Steps to Great Readers

1. Expect noise and plan for it. There is no such thing as silent reading in first grade. Learning to read is a loud, messy, noisy process. In order to sound out a word, students have to hear the sounds. As they begin to learn about punctuation, anything with an exclamation point at the end gets shouted with enthusiasm usually reserved for sporting events. You can mitigate the distracting effects of this noise with a technique I call "Divide and Conquer." Simply put, move the loudest readers to the farthest corners of the room. Some students have trouble regulating the decibel of their voice. Give them an elbow joint of PVC pipe, a "phonics phone," to read into. Whatever you do, don't tell them to be quiet. Their focus should be on making meaning of the words on the page, not learning to whisper or read in their heads. Those skills come later. What you hear first is the magical sound of learning to read.

2. Reward progress. Learning to read doesn't happen overnight. Often it is in excruciatingly small steps. Keep careful records of children's progress as they learn to read so that you can recognize progress and reward it. Nothing motivates a beginning reader more than getting a sense of his or her own progress. It makes the goal seem within reach and gives them that intrinsic motivation to continue the struggle. A simple comment like, "You knew those letters made the *ch* sound" or "You recognized that word from the other page" can help a student isolate and recognize the skills they are using. If they know what they are doing right, they are more likely to keep doing it.

3. Give them books they can read. Children learn to read by reading. That is the magical secret of reading and many other things in life (like teaching!). The only way to learn it is to do it. It follows, then, that students must be provided books at their individual reading level in order to make progress. If all the books are too easy, they are not learning. If all the books are too hard, they are frustrated. Assess your students often to make sure they are reading a slightly challenging book at their level. If they can read the whole thing fluently with no problems, they need a harder book. If they make more than five mistakes on a page, give them an easier book.

4. Keep it fun. I have a shelf in a locked cabinet in my classroom that contains something wonderful. It is a small collection of what I call "Special Books." Some are pop-ups, one has 3-D glasses, and they are out of the ordinary. If someone is not feeling well, loses a tooth, or got in trouble that morning and needs to get back on track, I call the student over and very quietly say, "Do you need a special book? Don't share it with anyone and bring it right back to me when you are finished." Never fails. Special books are fun.

5. Partners. Students need to be explicitly taught how to read with a partner. You may want to assign partners or somehow arrange that the partnerships are near the same reading level so that it is productive for both students. The guidelines should be discussed and developed as a class so that students understand the purpose of the exercise. They are not just reading for fun, they are helping each other to be better readers. For example, have them sit next to each other, not across from each other, so they can share the text. If there are two copies of the book, the partner needs to follow along with their finger in their book so they see the words as they hear them. Rules like these keep students on task and give their reading a purpose.

6. Groups. Children who are learning to read need an audience. Every once in a while they need to be heard. Put them in groups of three or four students to take turns reading to each other aloud. As with partner reading, establish rules and procedures about how to listen, give appropriate feedback, and take turns.

7. Location. Create spaces for "Serious Readers Only." Small children like to be under tables or desks, in pop-up castles or tents, and otherwise hidden from view. Sometimes we want to be alone when we are reading. As a teacher and a reader, I can respect that. I create nooks in my classroom by moving bookcases to allow space for one reader. I always give the space a name like "Special Reading Nook" and hang a "Do Not Disturb" sign somewhere.

8. Comfort. When I sit down to read a book, I rarely choose to sit with my feet on the floor at a desk with a straight-back chair. I want to curl up in a comfy chair or nook. I want a pillow on my lap to rest the book on or a pillow under my head. Give your students the same opportunity and they will exceed your expectations.

9. Systems and procedures. Students should know where their books are, which books they can read, where to find a bookmark, and when or if they can get up to get a drink or go to the bathroom. A classroom with clear procedures for how to use materials and move appropriately around the room is a place where students can become successful learners.

10. Snacks. Two saltine crackers work wonders when you want to keep students going through a long reading block. I can't stay focused when I am hungry, either.

CHAPTER 3

All for the Love of Reading

A Book Is a Gift

Pamela Jo Roller
Galveston, Indiana

The love of reading is the greatest gift a teacher can give students. To achieve this, students need ample opportunities to read for pleasure. Oftentimes, they read only what is required to get through their daily assignments. My second graders are given the first thirty minutes each morning all year long to read independently. They are allowed and encouraged to go to our school library every day. The students choose their own books to read. Many of the books are for *Scholastic*'s Reading Counts Program. This program holds my second graders accountable for their reading. The students read a book and then they take a quiz on the computer. They are asked five questions to check their comprehension, and a record is kept of the students' progress.

Not only does this increase reading comprehension scores, but it also holds students accountable for their reading and builds reading fluency.

My second graders are rewarded for earning points, and after achieving the number of points expected, they earn a very special T-shirt that I designed and had made at a local sporting goods store. For several years my students have strived to earn enough points to get a T-shirt. As a matter of fact, some of the students still wear their T-shirts even though the shirts are now too small and tight for them. Some of these students are now in the fifth and sixth grades.

Each Monday afternoon our whole school participates in DEAR time. DEAR is an acronym for Drop Everything And Read. All of our students in Grades K–6 and the staff members have their noses in books of their choice for fifteen minutes. Students witness adults reading, which is what they need to see modeled for them to become regular readers. This is a weekly practice we all look forward to.

So that no child is left behind, my students are provided with sixth-grade buddies. Each Monday and Wednesday morning for fifteen minutes, my second graders are paired with sixth graders to practice vocabulary words, high-frequency words, and to read together. When reading a story from our reader, a library book, or from a newspaper, the second graders and the sixth graders take turns reading. The sixth graders are trained to ask questions throughout the story or article being read. This is a win–win situation because my students receive individual help and they also get to hear the good expression used in the sixth graders' reading. Since 1991, this built-in weekly practice has truly helped my second graders. The sixth graders are continuously praised for being positive role models and for making a difference in another person's life. They are required to fill out an accountability sheet each time they work with my students. It is sent home with the second grader. The sixth graders are asked to write a few words of encouragement. This makes my students feel great and they are eager to try even harder. It keeps my second graders motivated to read.

I instill in my students the importance of making a difference in the world no matter what our age is. In 2003, I coordinated a project called "Recycle Our Books" for our entire school. The students and staff members were asked to part with books they had already read and were willing to give to a homeless child so they would have books of their very own to read. Six hundred used books (in good condition) were taken to the Emmaus Center for the homeless in Logansport, Indiana. When the boxes of books were delivered to the shelter, a few homeless young men helped carry in the boxes. I'll never forget what I witnessed. The young men started going through the boxes, like children opening birthday presents. They acted like the books were the greatest things they had ever seen. One young man picked up a book, opened it, and started reading it! He said, "Oh, this was my favorite book in school!"

To foster the love of reading, my students are given books as holiday gifts and again at the end of the school year as farewell presents. Reading is not just an important skill to be mastered. Instilling a love of reading in a child is a priceless gift.

Helpful Tips

■ Don't discard old, worn-out, used books or keep them stored in a forgotten place. Those books could be given to someone less fortunate to bring them the joy of reading. When the love of reading is passed on, it is truly a gift that keeps on giving!

CHAPTER *4*

Establishing a Summer Reading Program

Michele Rzewski Copeland

Sterling, Virginia

t has happened to all of us. . . . We have a student who started the school year barely reading at all. Then, after working with the child on phonics games and computer reading programs and literature-based activities, we get the child reading at grade level by the end of the school year, only to have parents refuse to place that child in summer school. How do we keep a struggling reader from losing reading skills over the summer? One of the ways to help is to have your school library host a summer reading program.

You may be wondering why you should set up a summer reading program at your school when your public library already hosts a summer reading program. Although public library programs are wonderful for encouraging students to check out books, they rarely track student performance in reading comprehension. They offer struggling readers little support in choosing "just right" books for supporting reading instruction. In my experience, summer reading programs at the public library also tend to serve the students who are already strong readers and who have parents with vehicles who can transport them to the library. A structured summer reading program that is school based can offer instructional reading support for struggling readers in ways that a public library program cannot. It can track a child's progress on reading skills and offer help to parents who want to work with their children at home on reading.

▣ What Should You Consider When Planning a Summer Reading Program?

Before establishing a summer reading program, it is important to analyze your school's population. It is essential that you identify which students you hope to reach with your program and that you determine measurable goals for those students. It is also essential to consider which community resources may be available to you (both in terms of human resources and financial resources). Finally, you need to identify partners who can help you with running your summer reading program. A summer reading program can be a lot of responsibility, and if you want to have time for a summer vacation, you really need to find someone to help you manage the sessions.

I am a librarian at a public K–5 elementary school in a suburb of Washington, D.C., and I am very fortunate to have two parent liaisons who work with me to run our summer reading program. Every year in March, we begin planning the summer reading program. We have divided the work load so that I am responsible for writing grants that fund the purchases of books for our summer reading program, and the parent liaisons are responsible for finding volunteers to staff our program. The parent liaisons send out promotional flyers to middle schools, high schools, and scouting organizations to find student volunteers who need to earn community service credit. I am responsible for training the volunteers to effectively buddy read with students and to use the Accelerated Reader program. Once we know approximately how many volunteers we will have, the parent liaisons begin to identify students who would benefit from participating in the program.

In planning a summer reading program, it is important to enlist the help of community businesses and foundations that can supply you with needed funds and motivational items. I have found that many businesses in the community are willing to provide food and motivational items if you write a letter of request well before the start date of your program. (The letter of request must explain exactly what is needed and why you need it, and it should be written on a school letterhead.) For instance, our program is funded primarily with grant money from the Loudoun Education Foundation and from ING Financial Services. We use grant money to purchase books, book bags, reading logs, audiobooks, and pencils for all our students. Our PTA funds online home access to the Accelerated Reader program. Wal-Mart and Costco supply our school with donated food, motivational prizes, and art supplies for story time. The county school system provides funds for student bus transportation once each week, and it pays one staff member (a parent liaison or school librarian) to be present at each meeting of the summer reading program. Funds from all these sources are essential for the smooth operation of the program.

How Do You Determine Who Should Participate in a Summer Reading Program?

My elementary school serves two diverse populations: upper-middle-class children with home access to computers and children of working-class recent immigrants who speak little English at home and who often travel to their home countries for a significant part of the summer. I have some students whose parents sign them up to participate in every possible school activity, and I have other students who never come to a single afterschool program. My challenge with designing a summer reading program was to create something that would meet the needs of struggling readers and the needs of high-achieving students who needed encouragement to continue reading during the summer.

To meet the needs of these two diverse groups, I designed a summer reading program that essentially has two parts: a program that is open for participation for all students and a special "invitation only" program for struggling readers. To promote the program that is open for all students, in June I meet with each K–4 class for a half hour to describe the program. I do a variety of book talks and show the students the kinds of arts and crafts they can make when they come to story time at the library during the summer. A calendar of the dates when the library will be open is distributed, and I hand out reading logs and bookmarks to all students. The Accelerated Reader prize incentive program is explained so students know they can earn small prizes for taking reading comprehension tests over the summer, and notices are sent home to parents about how they can help their children with reading skills over the summer by coming to the school library and using the online Accelerated Reader program. Students receive an informational brochure explaining that if they complete their summer reading log, they will receive a free used book and an invitation to a celebratory book party in the library in September. Additional publicity about the summer reading program is advertised on a sign in front of the school and is posted on the school Web site. Students do not need to sign up for this part of the summer reading program; they can "drop in" for scheduled story times and book checkout throughout the summer, or they can complete the reading log and Accelerated Reader quizzes entirely from home.

I am responsible for promoting the general summer reading program, and the parent liaisons are solely responsible for publicizing our specialized summer reading program for struggling readers. Students participating in the specialized portion of the program are usually in Grades K–3, are students who are identified by their classroom teachers as being in danger of losing reading skills over the summer without planned reading instruction, and are recommended for the program in May. The parent liaisons send home invitations and permission slips to the parents of these students, which are translated into the native languages of parents who do not speak English. As a follow-up, the parent liaisons call the parents of students who do not return permission slips. This part of the summer reading program is limited to thirty-five students. Enrollment is limited in this part of the program because bus transportation, food, and individualized reading instruction are provided to these students. Students who participate need to attend at least half of the six scheduled weekly sessions.

▧ What Does a Summer Reading Program Look Like?

Our school's summer reading program consists of six key components:

1. Buddy reading with trained middle and high school student volunteers

2. Use of the online Accelerated Reader reading comprehension program (both at school and at home)

3. Story time with art projects

4. Borrowing of school library materials, including cassette/CD players

5. Maintaining a reading log/parent communication log

6. Celebrating student accomplishments with awards and recognition

The targeted portion of the summer reading program lasts for six weeks during July and part of August. The students who participate in the specialized portion of our program are transported by school bus to the library each Monday for a two-hour session. When students arrive, they are given a healthy snack. Then the students meet with a middle or high school volunteer "reading buddy" who I have trained in basic reading instruction prior to the start of the program. Students select books to read with their reading buddy, and they read the books out loud. After reading each book, the students use the computer to take an Accelerated Reader reading comprehension test and vocabulary test on the book, and high school students print out score reports to communicate student performance on the tests to parents.

Students also record the books they have read in a reading log. They read and take tests on books for about forty-five minutes. Then I conduct a story time activity with the students for a half hour. At the conclusion of the story program, students and their high school reading partners work to create a craft related to the stories. The students use the craft as the focus for a story they write with the reading volunteers. At the end of the two-hour session, students may share their stories with each other and check out library books to read at home during the week. Students who are ESL students are invited to check out a cassette player and audiobooks to use at home to increase their English-language skills. They bring home their reading logs and Accelerated Reader test reports to their parents so they can see what their child read at the library, and reading volunteers are encouraged to write notes in a communication log describing the progress of the children to the parents.

While targeted students are invited to the summer reading program on Mondays, all other students at my elementary school are invited to come to the library summer reading program on Wednesdays and Fridays throughout July between 12:00 p.m. and 2:00 p.m. For this portion of the summer reading program, parents must provide transportation for the students, or students can walk to school themselves. When students come to the library, they can check out five library books. Students are invited to use the computer to take Accelerated Reader tests and can pick up prizes for points they have earned for taking reading comprehension tests at home. I often work with parents individually during these sessions to show them how the Accelerated Reader program works so they can track their child's progress with reading comprehension and vocabulary tests.

I also work with parents individually to show them how to find instructionally appropriate books for their children. Students are invited to attend a special story time presentation at 1:00 p.m., and they can create crafts related to the story time presentation. Parents are welcome to bring younger siblings not enrolled at the school to attend story time and check out books. The summer library visits serve as a great way to strengthen the home–school relationship and help parents to work with their children on reading instruction at home.

▧ Concluding the Summer Reading Program

When students return to school in September, they are encouraged to return their summer reading logs to the library. They are also encouraged to come to the library to pick up their Accelerated Reader incentive prizes for reading comprehension tests that they have taken over the summer. All students who return summer reading logs are invited to a special party in the library where students receive certificates and free used books. Students eat light refreshments at the party and talk with each other about their favorite books. The book party is a special event because all targeted students from the specialized summer reading program are invited to attend the party. It is exciting to see some of our neediest students attend a party alongside some of our top-performing students who always successfully complete things like reading logs.

Starting a summer reading program at your school library is not only a great way to keep your students reading over the summer. It is also a great way to get parents and caregivers to visit the school and become more involved in the education of their children. Students who participate in the summer reading program receive parent surveys asking parents for their opinions and feedback about the setup of the summer reading program. The following statements are summaries of parent comments. I am including them here for you to keep in mind when you plan your own program.

Positive Feedback From Parents

- They like the flexibility of the program. They like being able to come during weeks when it is convenient with their vacation schedule. Parents and caregivers like being able to bring younger siblings with them to story time.
- They like visiting the school library because the books in the school library have the reading levels marked so they can select instructionally appropriate books for their children, and they can ask the librarian for help in selecting books that relate to the science and social studies curriculum.
- They like the safety of holding the summer reading program events at the school library instead of at the public library, because they do not need to worry about strangers interacting with their children while they are reading with volunteers.
- They like having their children take Accelerated Reader comprehension tests over the summer at home and at school so they can see how much their children understand the books that they are reading.
- Parents of targeted students in the specialized portion of the summer reading program really liked having bus transportation

provided because their children could not have participated otherwise.

- Many wished that the program could have lasted for the whole summer instead of only six weeks.

Helpful Tips

Here are some great resources to help get you started:

- *Running Summer Library Reading Programs,* by Carole Fiore. New York: Neal Schumann, 1998.
- *Sizzling Summer Reading Programs for Young Adults,* by Katherine Kan. Chicago: American Library Association, 1998.

CHAPTER 5

Teaching Reading Strategies Through the Analysis of Visual Art

Susanne Burkhardt

Simpsonville, Kentucky

"It's a Picasso!"

"No, I'm sure it is a van Gogh. You'd think so too if you would just look at those big brush strokes. You know, van Gogh sure used a lot of paint. His paintings are always so thick."

"Hey, you might be right because I remember those brush strokes in Sunflowers*, and it was painted by van Gogh."*

—A conversation during the initial interaction with van Gogh's Café Terrace at Night

This is a conversation that occurred between two third graders in response to works of art. Sharing famous artwork is part of our daily schedule in Room 110 at Simpsonville Elementary. Students are introduced to a widely recognizable print each Monday. Through the week they learn about the print, the artist's style, the historical implications of the work, and the artist's life. I began this program with the intent to tie the content or subject of the prints to what the class was learning in content area studies. The program was born from the idea of increasing my students' integrated experiences with content learning. My hope was to provide additional avenues for understanding through multiple intelligences. But what have been most unexpected in this teaching endeavor are the reading skills and strategies that my third graders apply during their analysis of the art. The process by which they evaluate the art is very similar to the processes I am trying so hard to teach them to use with text when they are reading.

Integrating Art: Observations and Research

It is my experience as a classroom teacher that art brings content alive for students. My third graders have experienced a connection to immigration through creating tableaus using paintings that depict the historic times of immigration in the early 1900s, studying photos of Northwest Native American totem poles and creating their own to symbolize their lives, and using Greg Tang's book *MATH-Terpieces: The Art of Problem-Solving* to create number sentences from famous paintings. I have observed an increase in engagement, cross-curricula connections, and cognitive function in students when art is integrated into our curriculum.

I have witnessed how art gets to the heart of content. Students apply new knowledge quickly when they create a quilt, observe masterpieces to problem solve math riddles, bring the still images of an immigrant in a painting alive through "acting it out" in a tableau, or discuss the plant structures that are evident in *Red Poppy* by Georgia O'Keefe.

The Nuts and Bolts of "Art Connection" in My Classroom

Every Monday my third graders know there will be a large rectangular shape draped in a black satin cloth waiting for them in the front of the classroom. It is always the centerpiece of conversations in the room as students enter to start the week. "I wonder who painted it," "I think it's going to be a landscape because we are studying biomes," or "Can I peek, Mrs. Burkhardt? I promise I won't tell anyone." Monday is our "reveal day"—when students get to see our print of the week for the first time. When I unveil the print, I give the class 30 seconds to view it and then I turn it out of view. We discuss what they remember seeing, what stood out in the print, and their feelings about what they briefly saw. I introduce the name of the piece and the artist on Monday and why the print was chosen—what its connection is to what we are learning. This is a day for students to interact with the new print emotionally.

On Tuesday, we focus on the art objectives involved in the piece and any historical implication that the painting has. We add the artist and the painting to our Art Timeline on Tuesday. This enables students to see how this painting may have influenced or have been influenced by other artists and their works through a historical perspective. Wednesday is our day to study the author's life through Internet searches and literature. Mike Venezia's series *Getting to Know the World's Greatest Art* and *Smart About Art* have become favorites of my students.

Thursday we discuss the emotional implications of the piece, and on Friday we create something original inspired by our print of the week. But the one aspect that has overwhelmed me as a teacher, the one that was not planned and now happens every day of the week, is the manner in which my students employ reading strategies to analyze the art I introduced.

▧ "Reading" Art

Connections

> *"I have an art-to-self connection."*

> *"What is your connection?"*

> *"I went to the beach like those little girls last summer, and I wore a hat sort of like hers too . . . because my neck was sunburned."*

> *"That is a great connection and it helps you understand the picture even better. Yes, Mary Cassatt often paints hats in her pictures. And many of her pictures have children in them, so there are many connections kids can make to her work."*

Schema theory explains how our previous experiences, knowledge, emotions, and understandings affect what and how we learn (Harvey & Goudvis, 2000). All readers have schema, but as an elementary teacher, it is essential for me to model and teach my students how to access and apply their prior knowledge to text to increase both enjoyment and comprehension. Struggling readers often move through text without connecting the content of the reading to their lives, other texts, or the world in which they live. Struggling readers often do not "test" the text against what they already know to assure that it makes sense. Teaching children to connect reading to what they know is a great first strategy because every child has emotions, opinions, and personal experiences to which they can connect and make reading experiences more meaningful.

As with the example from the conversation about Mary Cassatt's *Children Playing on the Beach,* my students make quick connections to art that we can experience together. Without my prompting, students connect prints to their personal lives (text/print-to-self connection) to make meaning from them. This process creates the depth of thinking that I want my students to have when reading text. It is their true desire to make sense of something—to connect it to what we already know. The experience with the nonverbal artwork makes learning to connect easier for struggling students and more in-depth for advanced students. I am impressed with the depth of connection that students make when discussing our prints. I believe that it is the nonverbal nature of the art that speaks to them on an emotional level, and their connections pull the emotion out to gain meaning from the print—to assimilate it into what they already know. As we go deeper into our study of art and artists, students begin to make print-to-print connections much like the text-to-text connections I have modeled and taught during reading mini-lessons. In a recent study of the Mexican painter Diego Rivera, students compared *Baile en Tehauntepec* and *El Vendedor de Alcatraces*, which were introduced in different weeks. Although the paintings were created with different media and express very different emotions, students were able to connect them based on style and the expression of the artist.

A few weeks later, when we were engaged in a study of the author and illustrator Kevin Henkes, my students easily made connections between his texts: comparing writing style, characters, plot, and illustration techniques. Students were even interested in the publishing dates of the texts to compare how Kevin Henkes might have changed as he developed as a writer or may have been influenced by events in his own life or the world—much like our discussion of Diego Rivera and his development as a painter. Our experience with Diego Rivera and his art laid a foundation for the ability to discuss and analyze Kevin Henkes's craft as a writer and how we process and comprehend his work as readers.

My students have always had the most difficulty making text-to-world connections. I always attributed this to the fact that they have limited experience with current political and world events and what might be happening outside their neighborhood. We have learned in our study of art that art often stands within a historical perspective and frequently reflects the emotions of what may have been happening in the world at the time of its creation. For example, Pablo Picasso became very interested in the peace movement later in his life, and his work reflected the context of the world in the 1960s and his opinions and connections to it. I selected Picasso's *Dance of Youth* for my class to study because I felt it would support my community-building lessons at the onset of the year, but it also served as an excellent example of the print-to-world connection. We discussed how Picasso felt about the need for peace in the world. Students also saw this in *Guernica,* which depicts the Nazi Germany bombing of Guernica during the Spanish Civil War in 1937. When asked to make text-to-world connections in their reading, I can draw on the model of Picasso (and many other artists we've studied), whose artistic expression is often connected to the happenings in the world during his lifetime. Students fully understand this difficult concept first in a nonverbal setting before attempting it within text-based experiences.

Questions

"Do you think Ansel Adams really visited the Grand Tetons and the Snake River?"

"Of course. Mrs. Burkhardt said that he took that picture himself. He had to have been there."

"Oh yeah, this is a photograph. Is that really art, Mrs. Burkhardt?"

"I wonder if he was like on vacation there and saw that or if he went there just to take that picture. Do you think he took that from a helicopter?"

"What makes you ask that?"

"Well, look how high up it is and the trees look so small and the mountain and river are huge. That is like perceptive, right?"

"It is a perceptive thing to say, but I think you mean perspective, but you are on the right track."

Skilled readers approach text expecting to ask questions before, during, and after the reading experience. They anticipate using questions to understand and remember text. Appropriate questions guide the skilled reader to think, analyze, and sometimes reconsider what is being read. Proficient readers use self-questioning to actively engage in the reading process. They are looking for clarification and adjustment in their developing understanding of text. Struggling readers often think of questions only in terms of those that an outside source (teacher or test) may ask to check comprehension following reading.

Elementary-age children need to be taught to ask questions before, during, and after reading as a strategy to increase comprehension, enjoyment, and engagement in reading. Self-questioners have greater purpose in their reading and make text relevant and clear. Questioning has become a natural extension of making sense of art in my classroom. Students are full of questions about media used, color choices, inspirations, subject matter, artists' lives . . . all to gain greater meaning from the print they are interacting with for the week. My students are naturally curious, and self-questioning becomes a likely extension of their desire to know more about the print. It is interesting how their questions change through the week as they gain information, much like their questions change while reading. One strategy I use with art prints and text is to ask students to write questions before viewing and reading and again midweek or mid-reading. I also encourage them to go back and answer any of their previous questions as they gain knowledge through their interaction with the print and text. Students are also encouraged to ask their questions to classmates and family members to try to come up with an answer. I have found that questioning not only develops deeper comprehension but also increases engagement and purpose for children. It lets them control learning through their inquiry. Questions are based on what *they* want to know and clarify and eventually share with others.

Inferences

> *"It looks like maybe the artist was mad or scared when he painted that."*
>
> *"What clues make you think that?"*
>
> *"Can't you see those dark colors and how he swirled the paint around kinda 'crazy-like'? I think he was mad or frustrated and the colors are a little scary."*
>
> *"I love the way you used clues in the art to infer how the artist was feeling."*
>
> *—A conversation during interaction*
> *with Edvard Munch's* The Scream

One of the most difficult reading skills to teach young readers is how to infer meaning from text. It is a complex process for elementary-age students to "read between the lines" and find meaning. Inference requires a reader to synthesize what is known with what is implied to arrive at a new meaning. Inferring is really about developing insight. When a child is reading, she or he must think deeply about ideas, characters, plots, motivations, and personalities to make an inference. It can be difficult for students to see what is not there in text because they are looking for the answer to be stated. Art, due to its nonverbal nature, does not give the expectation of anything stated. Art demands inference because it is silent. There is no stated "correct answer" when discussing and analyzing art. My students become great detectives with art—collecting clues from the artist's life, color choice, brush strokes, subject matter, perspective, use of dark and light, and so on to bring meaning to the print.

As our week progresses with a print, my students develop in their thinking from prediction to inference. Initially students make predictions in regard to the print—solely using their background knowledge to make "guesses" about the meaning and purpose of a print. As they gather more information through the week, they begin to put the information together to infer meaning from the print. New knowledge learned about the artist, the time period of the art, the genre, and the reactions of classmates come together as the "clues" to uncovering meaning in the print.

Although inference continues to be a difficult skill for my third graders to master, practice with a nonverbal piece of art builds skills to collect information and to infer meaning based on prior knowledge and the implied. They better understand what inference is through art experiences because it is infrequent that the purpose of a piece of art is stated directly by the artist. In order to interact with a print, my students must infer meaning.

"Reading" Art in Your Classroom

When I share my ideas and strategies about art integration with teachers through professional development, I often am asked, "How can I make that happen in my room? I don't have all of those prints." I applied for and secured grant money to purchase prints, dry-mounting services, connected literature, and teaching resources, but these are not necessary to have a successful integrated art experience in your classroom. The Internet is a great resource for viewing famous artwork—simply use a search engine such as Google and search for "Images," and then use the Web to gather what you need. If you have projection capabilities with your computer or TV transmission from your monitor, you are set to begin! Also, if you have an art teacher or specialist in your school, she or he may have art posters that you could borrow for classroom use. Museums also have wonderful Web sites that provide viewing of artwork as well as background information one might need to delve deeper into the print with students.

The artwork I selected to share with my class was chosen for its connection to core content objectives. These connections are in addition to the reading objectives I have referenced in this chapter. By integrating art in many different ways, students' minds are open and are connecting content to increase understanding through different learning styles.

Matching Prints to Content	
The Persistence of Memory (Dali)	Time
Composition with Red, Yellow, and Blue (Mondrian)	Geometry
Autorretrato con collar de espinas y colibrí (Kahlo)	Writing Autobiographies
I and the Village (Chagall)	Communities
A Sunday on La Grande Jatte (Seurat)	Communities
Breakfast in Bed (Cassatt)	Families
The Starry Night (van Gogh)	Objects in the Sky/Space
The Flower Vendor (Rivera)	Economics
Composition (Pollock)	Symmetry (nonexample)
La Pont Japonais a Giverny (Monet)	Biomes (pond)
Goldfish (Matisse)	Basic Needs of Animals

Reference

Harvey, S., & Goudvis, A. (2000). *Strategies that work.* Portland, ME: Stenhouse Publishers.

CHAPTER 6

Using "Word Work" to Improve Decoding

Jennifer Ruth

Plano, Texas

When most people think of "word work," they think of spelling. The instruction of spelling patterns in many classrooms is kept completely separate from instruction in reading strategies. After working with many struggling students, I have found that effective word work lessons can be used to simultaneously improve the writing and reading of words. Spelling "programs" typically consist of a pretest on Monday, then a Friday quiz with few opportunities for direct instruction or exploration in between. Students frequently practice spelling by writing misspelled words several times. Repeated writing of misspelled words helps the child learn only one word at a time. If spelling is taught in isolation and reading strategies are not included, spelling becomes nothing more than an exercise in rote memorization. Worse yet, if the student continues to spell the word incorrectly, this practice becomes counterproductive. I believe there is a more efficient way to learn about words. Word work provides the opportunity to develop skills and achieve flexibility by manipulating letters and sounds to create meaning.

Although some of the English language follows no discernable pattern, there are some common threads woven throughout the language. Focusing on the patterns that occur most frequently allows students to apply every skill taught more accurately and consistently. All teachers realize the importance of maximizing instruction given the time constraints of the school day. I have discovered that students are more successful when the Monday spelling pretest is omitted in favor of quality word work throughout the week. This is a much more productive use of time. Combining spelling and decoding instruction helps students make powerful connections between reading and writing and doubles every effort made.

Even though many teachers do think of word study as synonymous with "spelling practice," word work consists of more than helping students understand how to put words together to create meaning. With some preparation and extension, these same lessons will enable students to take words apart and decipher unknown words in a text. Students need to be able to identify types of words, word parts, and chunks that represent meaning in order to decode a word. Early readers, kindergarten through third grade, are typically targeted for intensive instruction in word work. However, we have a tendency to overlook older children, who continue to need word study in areas such as common syllable patterns and root words. These students still encounter unfamiliar words in text that does not offer the variety of context clues found in lower-level reading. As passages become increasingly difficult, students realize that the strategies that have worked for them in the past are less often successful. A variety of strategies are necessary for upper elementary and middle school students to tackle more challenging texts.

Assessment

As with all meaningful activities, word work begins with assessment. Ask your students what they do when they are reading and come to an unfamiliar word. Your students will most likely answer, "I sound it out." This informal inventory identifies which skills your students feel most comfortable using. Unfortunately, when "sounding out" fails to help the child decode, the reader experiences frustration and the breakdown of comprehension. On the other hand, the best readers have a bag of tricks to use whenever they are challenged by a word. No one strategy works with all words, and we must provide our students with several tools to help them become independent readers.

You may already have completed a spelling or word-reading assessment with your students. A task such as this can be used to identify your students' strengths and weaknesses. Often teachers are required to do assessments at the beginning of the year, but we may not always use these assessments to help guide instruction or differentiate. The point of a diagnostic test is to diagnose the weaknesses the child may have so that lessons can be "prescribed" to fill in the gaps. My students drive instruction, and my analysis of their diagnostic assessments, spelling tests, and writing samples enables me to group students by areas of need.

▧ Getting Started

Once you have matched a group of students with a set of skills they need to build, you are ready to begin planning a lesson to target their needs.

Some possible topics of word study include:

short vowels

long vowels

word families (*-ink, -ong, -ain*)

prefixes

suffixes

proper nouns

syllable patterns (open, closed)

common syllables (*-tion, -ture*)

Latin root words

To help students experience success early and promote later perseverance, I suggest teaching the easiest skills first. For example, a group of students who need to master prefixes and long-vowel–silent-letter *e* patterns should work on long vowels first since they occur more frequently and follow a pattern. The targeting of instruction in this manner allows you to teach only the skills the students need when they are ready to learn them.

Making Words

I have found that the routine of a "making words" lesson is a good venue for word study. This word work lesson enables students to recognize chunks of words they already know, which helps build success. When students learn to break a word into manageable pieces, they are much more likely to decode the word independently. This is the basis for many good reading strategies. Typically, in a making words lesson, students are given a specific set of letters. They make as many words as they can with this set of letters and eventually create a "mystery word" using all of the letters. What separates a truly productive making words lesson from one that merely asks students to perform rote tasks is the discussion and extension you provide for your students. Effective extension takes planning and preparation on your part and yields an enriching experience for your readers.

To begin with, select a mystery word that will enable you to teach the targeted skill. For example, if the goal is to work on prefixes, select a word that either has a prefix or contains the letters necessary to make one or two prefixes. If you are targeting vowel pairs, choose a word with several vowels. Mystery words are usually seven or more letters long, as this provides many letters to work with. Although there are many ways to organize manipulative letters, I believe that providing small sets of only the letters necessary for the lesson preserves the time allotted for student learning.

This extra step is well worth the additional preparation. After all materials are distributed, ask the students to make as many two- or three-letter words as possible. Starting with a simple and clear expectation will help your slower starters to feel successful. Having students write the words that they make connects the manipulative to spelling and provides a basis for discussion. The students will continue creating four-, five-, and six-letter words, eventually discovering the mystery word, which can be made using all the letters. As the students are manipulating letters, I discuss the words they are creating. This step, which is often ignored, is vital to ensuring that students are focusing on the skill you need to target. This is when I ask my students questions to make connections to both reading and writing.

"Your word is a person's name. How would we write that in a story?"

"Alicia has made the word *map* with *-ap*. How can this word help you read the word spelled *f-1-a-p*?"

"Michael has made the word *sing*. Can anyone make a different word with *-ing*?"

"Josh made the word *late*. Angie made the word *plate*. Those two words rhyme. Can anyone make another word that rhymes with *late* and *plate*?"

"If you can spell *pink,* can you spell *blink,* or *think,* or *wrinkled*?"

This discussion is what elevates the manipulation of letters to a higher level of cognition. During this conversation, the targeted skill or pattern is introduced.

Read, Write, and Spell

Traditionally, the making words lesson ends with the creation of the mystery word. However, to help students connect this pattern to text, students need opportunities to read, write, and spell the pattern. Direct the students' focus to the word part you have selected to target. Discuss the words the students have already found that fit the pattern. My kids love using highlighters to find the focus words on their paper. Explain to students how knowing the pattern can help them to read and spell other words. Guide them to recall other words that fit the pattern. Writing down these new words reinforces this connection. If a student seems reluctant to take a risk, I will demonstrate how to add consonants or blends to the beginning or end of chunks to create new words. Encourage students to "try out" these combinations aloud, since saying the sounds, hearing the sounds, and writing the ones that make sense all combine to engage more areas of the brain than any one method.

To help your students connect back to text, have them locate words in books that have the same targeted word part. Point out how knowing the pattern helps them to read these words. To turn knowledge of this new skill into a decoding strategy, prepare some larger words with the same imbedded pattern. For example,

Query:	What is the pattern?
disable	dis-able
wrinkle	wr-ink-le
spider	sp-i-der
listlessness	list-less-ness

Students should first locate the pattern in the word and then add the surrounding letters to decode the word. Provide multiple opportunities for the group to isolate the pattern. I often ask my students to find creative ways to show me the pattern, and they amaze me with their strategies. Words written on strips of paper can be cut into parts. If the words are typed, the font can be changed to "outline." This will allow the students to color in the pattern with crayons. A frame can be built around a pattern segment either with a card that has a hole cut out or just using your fingers. Visually isolating one section of a word is particularly successful for students who may see letters moving on the page. Students with dyslexia or learning disabilities find this strategy helpful.

Finally, to relate the pattern to spelling, remove all the examples you have been working with from view. Give students some words they may not have discussed but that fit the pattern. Ask them to write or build these words. Remind students that if they can spell *pink,* for example, they should be able to spell *think, drink,* and *clink.*

As with all concepts, you will need to review the pattern from time to time. I like to review by throwing in a few words from a previous pattern while I am asking them to spell a new pattern. This trains their ears to listen for the differences between how words sound. By this point, your students have had many opportunities to practice the targeted skill in different ways, which helps them internalize the pattern, not memorize just one word. Focusing on the commonalities of words allows students to make connections and not rely on memorization as in traditional spelling programs. Your students will become successful at reading and spelling any word they encounter that fits the targeted pattern.

🗞 Other Ideas

When thinking about patterns to present to your groups, consider more than just spelling. Think about how commonalities of the language can help students more effectively gain meaning from text. For example, one of the first skills I teach third graders is how to recognize proper nouns. It seems to be the case that even though students have been taught how to write proper nouns, they are unable to pick out proper nouns in text without additional instruction. If you have ever heard an elementary student try to decode a word like *Pflugerville,* you know how important recognizing proper nouns can be. I teach my students to find proper nouns and then use context clues to decide if the noun labels a person, place, or thing. Once students have discovered what the word identifies, I tell them to take a guess as to the pronunciation of the name or choose a replacement word like *Bob.*

We talk about how many names of people and places do not follow any patterns and how American English has borrowed words from other languages. I tell them that when I read about dinosaurs or Native American groups, I often just have to take a guess and continue to read for meaning. This has really helped my students to improve their fluency of text without negatively impacting their comprehension. In fact, in most cases comprehension is improved with this strategy since students do not get bogged down with trying to "sound out" words that are not phonemically regular.

After my students learn several different strategies for decoding words, we play word guessing games like "blank." I prepare sentences with a blank for certain words. I give the students clues such as the beginning sound, a suffix, or a word pattern found in the word. Students brainstorm a list of possible words to fill in the blank based on sentence meaning. They narrow down the list as they get each new clue about how the word looks and sounds. The students go back to the beginning of the sentence and reread the sentence to get a "running start." I give them the analogy of jumping over a large puddle. To jump over a puddle, you can't stand on the edge and jump; you have to back up to get a running start. To cross over a difficult word, you also have to back up and get a running start in order to make it to the other side. Rereading the sentence several times helps the student focus on the meaning of an unknown word. Clues about the construction of the word help students focus on their knowledge of how words work. Although students think this is fun, it is a realistic reenactment of what good readers do when they come to a challenging word.

Each of my students has a bookmark that serves as a visual reminder of the many strategies they have been taught to help them read an unfamiliar word. We begin every reading session by reviewing these strategies so that the students are prepared to tackle unknown words. Once students have had many opportunities to practice with each strategy, they internalize the strategies as skills of a good reader.

Helpful Tips

- Planning and preparation are the keys to making any lesson successful; specifically, the management of materials for word work requires particular attention. Have the specific letters necessary for the lesson prepared as well as a list of any words you want to make sure to discuss with the students. You can use commercially available letter tiles, magnetic letters, or index cards for manipulatives. I have found that the easiest way to prepare a specific set of letters for a lesson is to type them on a spreadsheet program. I can make a row of the letters I need and copy and paste it as many times as I need to. It is faster for me to cut these letters apart for each group than it is to look through letter tiles to pick out the letters necessary for each child. In addition, this way, you can send the letters home with the students for extra practice.

- For kindergarteners and first graders who are not quite ready for making words, you can do activities that involve the manipulation and comparison of letters. For example, you can use alphabet stickers in different fonts and have students sort the letters. Young children often have difficulty identifying some letters when they are written in an unusual font. Sorting helps students discriminate the important features of each letter.

- When you first begin word work lessons, they will take some time. Some teachers prefer to do the first few lessons with the whole

(Continued)

(Continued)

class. This provides an opportunity for them to understand your expectations and gain some automaticity. Once your students are accustomed to the basic routine, you will want to begin doing word work in smaller groups in order to target instruction to student need. Eventually you will be able to do a word work lesson with a small group in ten to twenty minutes.

■ You can find an endless number of word work activities in professional books and online for all grade levels. Remember to select activities that provide opportunities to connect reading and writing. A student who understands how words work will be a successful reader and writer.

CHAPTER 7

Reading Aloud

Comprehending, Not Word Calling

Jenna Hallman

Anderson, South Carolina

Reading is a fundamental goal that children must master in order to be successful in school and in life. As professional educators, we know that. Parents, principals, district leaders, and even our government are constantly pushing us to increase the reading levels of the students in our classrooms. To many, reading has become a number that simply depicts a level of achievement rather than a complex process. Reading instruction has narrowed so that the goal is only to have a child reading at their grade-specified level. My belief is that these children are not reading; they are calling words and there is a significant difference.

The act of reading is a sophisticated mesh of many different individual skills. It includes the reader's ability to problem solve and decode unknown or unfamiliar words, phrase passages, add expression and tone as appropriate, and create a fluent dialogue, all of which allow them to comprehend the complexities and the subtleties of what is being read. When these acts become seamless instinctive maneuvers, we may then say that the child is reading. A child who is perfectly calling the words from the page without appropriate phrasing and in a monotone voice is not actually reading. They are missing several of the key components, and this will affect their comprehension of the text.

Fluency, expression and tone, phrasing, and *decoding* are terms thrown around carelessly by reading teachers everywhere. There are many established definitions I could pull and cite in this document. I have chosen instead to explain them in my own words and try to give a picture of what they look like in an elementary classroom. Fluency refers to the ability to read effortlessly. Fluent readers sound as if they are carrying on a conversation. They do not use a staccato style. Real fluency is achieved only when decoding, phrasing, and expression are mastered.

Expression refers to the reader's ability to add feeling and emotion to the text. Expressive readers use a toolbox of emotional voices, as well as facial expression, to convey the character or author's feelings. When readers phrase appropriately, their brain places larger quantities of words together. The result is a lyrical, almost rhythmic sound rather than short, punctuated segments of words. Finally, decoding is the problem-solving aspect of reading. It includes the use of syntax, meaning, and visual discrepancy to decipher unfamiliar words. Readers must have an arsenal of strategies that they comfortably employ when they stumble upon a difficult word.

You have probably noticed that I failed to discuss comprehension in the preceding paragraph. The reason is because comprehension, or the understanding of a text, is the natural by-product of fluent, expressive, and well-phrased reading. When children are focusing all of their attention on decoding words, their brain is overworked and cannot comprehend what they are reading. There are strategies that I teach for the purpose of improving comprehension, but many of them become unnecessary when true reading is taking place.

In my classroom, reading instruction is a huge portion of my day. My district has currently adopted the balanced literacy approach to reading instruction. This means that I teach reading at three different times. During the interactive reading piece, I model expression, tone, phrasing, and therefore true fluency as I read a book aloud to the class. The books are carefully chosen to represent a wide variety of genres, levels, and authors. I begin by summarizing the book and having the children make and support their predictions. The children must be able to identify a picture clue and make a connection to a personal experience or to an author's previous work to support their prediction.

I then give the children a purpose for reading and remind them to listen for examples of fluency. Depending on the length and topic of the book, I stop two or three times to model a comprehension strategy. The students and I work together to determine cause and effect, draw a conclusion, make an inference, or identify a literacy element. When the book is finished, the children identify specific examples of fluency including changes in my voice, phrasing, and facial expressions.

The second piece of the balanced literacy program is shared reading. During this activity, every child must have access to the text. This means that each child has a copy of the book in their hands, that we are reading a big book, or that the text is on a chart or on an overhead. During shared reading, we have opportunities to work on fluency as well as practice decoding and further develop comprehension strategies. I often use poetry during my shared reading time. The lyrical nature of poems really improves the students' phrasing. We begin by identifying the text features such as commas, periods, exclamation points, questions marks, and quotation marks.

I have the children explain how these text features will affect their reading. They begin by reading the poem to themselves. As they read, they highlight troublesome words with a yellow crayon. After a quick glance at individual papers, I choose two or three highlighted words to model decoding. The next step is to read the poem chorally at our tables. This gives the children an opportunity to establish their phrasing and expression. Finally, we read the poem as a class. We use our comprehension strategies to discuss the poem. My decision to provide the children with three opportunities to read the poem is deliberate. The first attempt focus is on decoding. The second attempt is to work on phrasing and expression (fluency). The final read is the mesh of all the processes and the presentation of the final product. The students keep each poem we read in their poetry folder at their desk for future rereading, which is another great way to develop fluency.

The third component of balanced literacy is the guided reading piece. In guided reading, my children are flexibly grouped based on their established reading level. I use the term *flexibly grouped* because my reading groups are not stagnant. A child can move in and out of groups as their reading improves and based on their individual needs. I use groups of no more than six children and no less than three children for guided reading. During a typical lesson, the children join me to read a leveled text that I selected for them based on the previous day's work. I examine their needs as well as their strengths and choose books that allow them opportunities to use both.

I start by summarizing the story as the children picture-walk the story. They make and support their predictions based on what they see during their picture walk. We set a purpose for reading and begin. If the children can read in their heads, everyone begins at the same time, and I tap individual children when I want them to read out loud. If the children are still reading aloud, I stagger starting them so that not everyone is at the same point at the same time. As I listen to each individual child, I guide them to employ decoding strategies, make anecdotal notes, and praise their attempts at fluency, expression, phrasing, and decoding. When everyone has completed their reading for the day, I choose one comprehension strategy to teach. We utilize that strategy as a group to determine the main idea or whatever my focus skill is. Finally, we choose a book the group read in a previous lesson and reread a few pages of the familiar text to further establish fluency.

Reading is a complex process that must be modeled, taught, practiced, and evaluated on a daily basis. It includes the ability to decode words as well as appropriate phrasing, tone, expression, and fluency. These interrelated components form the bridge that allows the reader to comprehend the text in hand. Calling words in staccato fashion is not reading and cannot be accepted as such. As professional educators, we must strive to teach our children to be true readers. If we can succeed in this area, we will truly have reached our goal of developing lifelong readers.

Helpful Tips

- Poems can often be sung in a round fashion. If the round ends correctly, the teacher will know that the children were truly reading with fluency.
- When working on comprehension have your children "prove" their answers. Have them reread a sentence from the text, point out a

picture clue, or explain the personal connection that helped them answer the question. This keeps children from making snap decisions.

- Give the students plenty of time to reread familiar texts to develop fluency. Teachers can always establish a new purpose for rereading a text.
- Use the term "fluent reading" with the children. Model it and explain what it means. Show them the difference between "robot reading" and "fluent reading."
- When you as the teacher make a mistake in your reading, stop and model a decoding strategy. Did you use meaning, structure, or syntax to correct your mistake?
- Allow older readers to read to younger readers. This creates an authentic reason to read. The better the fluency and expression, the better the attention!
- Discuss the interrelatedness of reading and writing with the class. The more you write, the better you read, and vice versa.

CHAPTER 8

Comprehension

Making Connections to Text

Linda Hennen

Blacksville, West Virginia

The benefit of making connections is what the children gain in understanding from thinking about what they are reading. That is why many children can't comprehend text. Have you ever read a book and realized you had no idea what you just read? All you did was read words; no meaning came from the words. Children must make high-quality, relevant connections about the text to make meaning of their reading. This doesn't just happen; they have to think about what they are reading. This enables them to make higher-level connections and have a deeper understanding of the text. They are then able to move beyond mere shallow understanding. When a child thinks about the text and internalizes the material, it is only natural for them to want to talk about it. Have you ever read a really good book and couldn't wait to tell a friend about it?

My first thoughts on "Making Connections" were not favorable. "You want me to encourage students to talk! You want me to waste my instructional time listening to their stories!" I spent a great deal of my day telling my first graders to "be still, raise your hand, and we need to move on." When my small rural school in West Virginia received a Comprehensive School Reform (CSR) Grant, the staff spent days researching best practices and selected Making Connections as a school-wide reform. Making Connections is linked to multiple researched-based practices for building comprehension. Step one was a book study using Debbie Miller's *Reading with Meaning*. This book inspired me to change the way I see my classroom environment and my role as a teacher.

Text-to-Self Connections

Text-to-self connections are highly personal connections made between the reader/listener of a written text and the reader's/listener's own life experiences (schema). Very young students gain a deeper understanding of a text when they can make authentic life connections. These connections or responses allow the readers to become involved with the story. They feel like the characters and can place themselves within the story, therefore making more connections to the story.

On the very first day of first grade, I read to my students *No, David!* and *David Goes to School* by David Shannon. As I read each book, I modeled making text-to-self connections by using a "Think Aloud" strategy. "Look at this picture; I can remember when my sons played with their food at the dinner table." "Oh my, I remember when. . . ." "He acts just like. . . ." "Yesterday someone in the cafeteria did the same thing." The students could relate to David getting into trouble at home and at school. They shared stories about themselves by going back to the things David did and sharing their own escapades.

The next day, during a read-aloud, *Chrysanthemum* by Kevin Henkes, I introduced the terminology *text-to-self connections*. Once again using a "Think Aloud," I modeled making the connections. "I have a text-to-self connection with Chrysanthemum; I always wished my name was something else." Everyone had something to share about their names or someone being mean to them. The success of this introduction to using text to-self connections was closely related to the choice of good text. They were able to relate closely to David and Chrysanthemum. Selecting high-quality literature is of the utmost importance for making eager, meaningful connections. It was evident that they were beginning to think about their reading, and my new teaching technique was deepening their understanding.

🔖 Text-to-Text Connections

Making text-to-text connections is my favorite comprehension strategy. I love children's literature and the insight, understanding, and logic of how children interpret these stories. Every year someone sees something new in a story that I have read for years. How can they do this? Every one of us brings a completely unique set of experiences with us to each read-aloud. Each student's schemata, his or her different cultural and linguistic background, affects their perception of each story. Making text-to-text connections is looking for the commonalities between a new story and a previously read story. The first piece of children's literature I read to model this strategy was *The Three Little Pigs*. (We continue to make text-to-self connections with this story.) The next piece of literature was *The Three Little Wolves and the Big Bad Pig* by Helen Oxenbury. These two stories have the same characters and setting with a reverse problem, and they lend themselves to making connections. As I modeled what I was thinking, I talked about both stories having pigs. One little boy said, "They both have THREE pigs." The class immediately moved into the new strategy.

There are many "Three Little Pig" stories, and after I read them, I display them around the room for the students. Sometimes they use the titles to make the connections, other times they describe the cover, the characters, or the plot to explain the two books they are using to make connections. Some of the students touch each book. Some of the less proficient students use pictures, colors, and numbers to make connections. Other students use higher levels of thinking and demonstrate the use of inferring and synthesizing to make this comprehension connection. Another set of books is *The Wolf Who Cried Boy* by Bob Hartman and *The Boy Who Cried Wolf* by Keiko Kasza. Students are able to comprehend and synthesize the boy crying wolf and apply that knowledge to connect with the wolf crying boy.

We transitioned from *The Three Little Pigs* to *Cinderella*. The story line or plot of *Cinderella* is more complex. I read *Cinderella* and *Cindy Ellen* by Susan Lowell. There are many Cinderella stories. This is wonderful to use with older students. The students now make connections without being asked; it is part of their vocabulary and everyday activities. They make connections in math, during writing, and even during recess. I hear the students independently discussing connections during self-selected reading time and on the reading rug. They discuss their guided reading books, the stories their mom reads to them at bedtime, and the stories we read together. They pretend they are the teachers and others will be students. The teacher always asks for connections. They connect what they had for lunch with their dinner the night before.

It was time to assess their understanding of what they are doing. "How do you think making connections will help you as a reader?" They all just looked at me! Then one little boy slowly raised his hand. I was certain I was not going to get a deeper level of understanding from this less proficient child. Very slowly he said, "If you can see one picture in your head, then it is easier to see another." Talk about metacognition: this child knew how his mind worked! I was the one out there in left field. Someone else shared that making text-to-text connections helped you guess what would happen next in a story. I am a believer. They understood, applied, and synthesized. We moved on.

I gave each child a large sheet of paper, and they folded it in half. On this paper they had to select a connection between the two stories, write it, and draw the picture to match. Then we shared. Everything was accepted and applauded. All levels of understanding, comprehension, and skill level were apparent. The next activity we tried was T-Charts. A T-Chart is a comparative writing activity that can be used to list how the two books are the same or different. We completed a T-Chart on two Cinderella stories, *Cinderella Big Foot* by Mike Thaler and *Big Foot Cinderella* by Toney Johnston and James Warhola. On chart paper, we listed things from both stories. Some of the commonalities were shoes, a prince, someone mean, Cinderella, and a fairy. Once again they took ownership of this activity and ran with it. Just give a first grader a partner, a marker, and a full sheet of chart paper and they will amaze you. I chose the set of partners, matching higher and lower skills for this first charting activity. I wanted to make sure each group would be able to complete the activity.

Usually the higher-skilled students are the leaders. The two levels working together offered each child what they needed to complete this new activity through peer teaching. When everyone was finished, we shared in whole group. The sharing was wonderful. There were a lot of lightbulbs going on, and the positive reinforcement was coming from their classmates. The next time we did this activity, I grouped them with equal or close skill levels. I wanted to make sure everyone had the opportunity to grow. Students need to apply a wide range of strategies to comprehend texts. They draw on their prior experiences, interactions with text, and their ability to communicate this to others. Teacher modeling, vast amounts of practicing, and fine-tuning using making connections allow students to become proficient with reading comprehension. The enrichment and engagement with high-quality children's literature give students opportunities to communicate and share their unique understandings. Student success with reading can be achieved with the use of Making Connections.

Text-to-World Connections

The text-to-world connections are the larger connections students make about how the world works. These connections go far beyond our own personal experiences. This strategy is more difficult for first graders. I found that the best materials to use are student newspapers written on grade level. The topics are world-centered, current events but written on a first-grade level of understanding. Content area subjects are also useful when applying understanding of text-to-world connections. We make safety posters for our local business partners and make connections with safety at school and at home.

We discuss our classroom rules and link them to adult rules and the need for rules. The most powerful topic for text-to-world connections is our "Famous American Unit." Each student reads about a famous person and presents their information to their peers and parents. The best example of success became apparent when the students realized that Abraham Lincoln and Harriet Tubman must have lived during the same time in history. They also questioned when Rosa Parks lived and how different it is now. Sometimes making a text-to-world connection is a struggle for younger students. I would love to see what upper grades could do with making connections. Text-to-world connections could make any topic come alive with students of any age. Just think of the themes, research, interaction, and communication skills that are used while making comprehension connections with literature. I am sure they could draw the parallels between the text and the outside world with distinctive insight available only to teens of today's culture.

During the second year of the grant, my first-grade students already had the vocabulary and the foundation for making connections in their schemata. They were ready to start making connections on day one. When students recognized and practiced these three kinds of textual connections, they grew in their abilities to understand and comprehend text and context while thinking and talking about their connections. They can take ownership of literature and of their learning. Making connections enables teachers to meet the students at their level of learning and scaffold the instruction to meet individual needs. Each year I grow in my ability to facilitate this strategy, and I gain a deeper understanding of my students.

Helpful Tips

Text-to-Self Questions:

- What does this remind me of?
- What is this like in my life?
- Has something like this happened to me?

Text-to-Text Questions:

- What does this remind me of in another book?
- How is this book like another book?
- Have I read about something like this before?

Text-to-World Questions:

- What does this remind me of in the real world?
- How is this book like things that happen in the real world?
- How does this matter to me in the real world?

CHAPTER 9

Incorporating Drama and Writing

Performing a Mystery Play

Summer Williams

Auburn, Alabama

I believe in using drama in the classroom because I see it create sparks within even the most hesitant reader. It is a personal goal as a teacher that my students develop a love of reading, and that can't be done if I'm not making reading pleasurable and relating it to their everyday lives.

I teach all of the standards by grouping objectives into big genres. We immerse ourselves in the genre and then create our own example of the genre through writing pieces, puppet shows, plays, wax museums, and so on.

My students have shown me that the biggest incentive I can give them is a goal to work for in which they can strut their knowledge.

When they know the culminating activity is a chance to perform in front of a group, they strive for the best!

This activity—the performance of a mystery play—is a creative way for kids to use drama in the language arts classroom. This unit can be very extensive or quite brief, depending on your time constraints. As long as they are able to read the script, then the students should be able to participate. The script can be adapted to meet all grade levels and can be used as improvisation with a little coaching.

I bought the play for the following lesson from www.merrimysteries .com for $30. (For other sources, see the Helpful Tips.) They e-mail the script immediately and you can save it to your computer, which is a huge organizational time-saver for me! There are different scripts to choose from. I personally have used *Mystery in the Library* for sixth graders and *Who Stole the Cookies* for second graders. Both of these plays use fairy-tale characters, great for culminating activities for a fairy-tale unit. The mystery party will take one class period of about 90 minutes. The prerequisites leading up to this lesson can take many days, depending on time constraints.

To prepare for the mystery party, the students should take a few days (I suggest a week) to familiarize themselves with the literature. They can do this by partner reading, individual reading, group reading— whatever you prefer.

First, allow the students to sign up for the character they wish to play. You may want to send a parent letter home explaining the lesson and inform them that they do not need to go out and buy costumes, but to be creative.

The students are given their mystery pages (which will inform them of what they need to reveal during each scene). They will also be given the script to read. The mystery can be done in two ways (depending on grade level and preference). Either have the students read the script aloud as a whole class (in a circle seems to work best) or cut up the clues and have the students meet and mingle to find out the information they need to solve the crime.

At the end, the students write who they believe is guilty on a secret ballot. They also write who they believe has the best costume. (I give prizes for who is closest to the correct person and motive as well as whom the class agrees has the best costume.) The teacher reads all motives before reading the "Who Did It?" page.

Helpful Tips

Additional ideas for incorporating writing and more drama into your Fairy-Tale unit (which are endless!):

- The students can write a fairy-tale tabloid magazine. Publish it!
- The students can write a fairy-tale newspaper that includes classi-fieds, a television guide, top stories, a crime report, and so on.
- Pick three characters and write fifty words about the charac-ter's personality. In groups, develop other characters.
- The students can collaboratively write their own mystery script to act out.
- Extend the play with a court scene. Have students write a script and act out how the culprit will be punished.
- Illustrate wanted posters for the missing book and/or culprit.
- Buddy journal with each other's character.
- Perform radio shows or newscasts on the "special report" of the mystery.
- Use photo journals with pictures of the students in costume.
- Find other plays to do in your classroom.

The following Web sites are sources of other great ideas for incorpo-rating drama and writing in your classroom:

- http://www.aaronshep.com/rt/RTE.html

This is a free Web site offering Tall Tale plays—great for a Tall Tale unit.

- http://www.gigglepoetry.com/

When you click on the link Poetry Theatre, you will find many poems for your class to perform!

- http://www.badwolfpress.com/

This company prides itself on providing the music and the script with suggestions for doing a play, especially for teachers with no experi-ence. I have used *Turkeys on Strike* with second graders and it was really low-key and easy! Most plays cost $39.95.

- http://www.playsmag.com/

Here you can order a subscription that sends seven issues a school year for $39.00. This magazine has an average of nine plays for mostly middle and upper grades on a wide variety of themes.

■ http://www.broadwayjr.com/default_HOME.asp

If you have a big budget and would like to put on a bang of a show, choose Broadway Junior plays. For approximately $600.00, the company will send you the following for putting on a play: the director's script, a production handbook, a vocals book, twenty scripts for the cast, and a choreography video. I used these with the drama club I started at the middle school where I taught and charged a small fee for each participant. It's a big job, but the outcome is really worth it!

CHAPTER 10

Social Studies

Reading About Life in the 1800s

Donna Bradley

Mobile, Alabama

This unit, developed to connect reading and social studies, compares modern-day living to life in the 1800s. The learning environment for my students is transformed into a classroom of the 1800s. We begin by gathering materials such as a replica of a covered wagon, a washboard, some antique milk jugs, a few handmade quilts, hand-carved wooden toys, and anything I could find from that period.

Although reading was the main focus of the unit, I discovered how easy it is to integrate other subjects. Children's literature was collected from the school and classroom libraries, local libraries, and books purchased from bookstores. During my search for literature with the help of the Internet, I found a series of picture books, "My First Little House Books," adapted from the "Little House Books" by Laura Ingalls Wilder. The books are perfect for second graders. The pictures are beautiful.

One of the books, *Going West,* was used as a read-aloud to introduce the characters and setting of the series. Graphic organizers were used to display the relationships of the characters in the story. This is a great way for students to make connections with their own family and the life of a child in a pioneer family. A Venn diagram helped students compare and contrast their home and community to the homes and communities of long ago.

The unit can be taught in two to four weeks, depending of the depth of the study. Students engaged in role-playing—packing a covered wagon, a table top, with items needed for the long journey. Music was incorporated into the unit as students learned square-dancing techniques while singing along with favorite pioneer songs. Graphing favorite complementary colors, an excellent math lesson, led to measuring construction paper to create a class quilt using the favorite complementary colors.

Using whipping cream, yellow food coloring, a pinch of salt, a two-minute timer, and some small jars, students worked in pairs to make butter. They labored together to put the ingredients into the jars, secured the lids, and took turns shaking the jars. As one student shook the jar, the other student set the timer. When time was up, students changed roles and repeated the process until the cream had turned to butter.

This exciting hands-on science lesson made students aware that a liquid can change to a solid. Paper and pencils were not used during our pioneer study; instead, students used small chalkboards and chalk to complete lessons. Classroom visitors were greeted as students stood and addressed them with a well-mannered greeting. Physical education period became recess, and students were allowed to play with marbles and jump ropes. During reading time, each student read orally using many books on a variety of levels.

Helpful Tips

Read a variety of literature. These are some sources we find useful:

Harcourt Brace Social Studies textbook, Unit 6, People in Time and Places, pages 218–221, 224–227.

(Continued)

(Continued)

The "My First Little House Books," adapted from the "Little House Books" by Laura Ingalls Wilder.
The following books:

- Laura Ingalls Wilder books
- *An Author's Story* by Sarah Glasscock
- *Prairie Primer A to Z* by Carolina Stutson
- *My Great Aunt Arizona* by Gloria Houston
- *The Josefina Story Quilt* by Bruce Degen
- *The Patchwork Quilt* by Valerie Flournoy

CHAPTER *11*

Social Studies

Reading the Vietnam Memorial Wall

Donna Bradley

Mobile, Alabama

I n this lesson, students learn about a national monument, the Vietnam Memorial Wall. I start by activating students' prior knowledge by using a KWL (What I KNOW, What I WANT to Know, What I LEARNED) chart. I want to find out what the students already know about the Vietnam Memorial Wall and what they want to learn. According to the students' abilities, they write their ideas on sticky notes or I write their ideas as dictated. After brainstorming, I read *The Wall,* by Eve Bunting, to the class. After the story, the students add to the KWL chart by saying what they learned from the book. We discuss the author's purpose and identify characters' feelings. Open-ended questions are used to allow students to make connections, text-to-self, text-to-text, and text-to-world. Students write their feelings about the story in their reading journals and meet in small groups to read and discuss their entries.

The next day, we revisit the book and discuss how to write letters to our local veterans and soldiers. We review the parts of a friendly letter and brainstorm a list of words students may need during their writing. The writing process is used, and when the finished product is ready for publishing, students share their letters with the whole group before we mail them to the prospective veterans.

The book *The Wall* lends itself well to review high-frequency words, words with inflectional endings, and compound words. Teaching mini-lessons using familiar text is an excellent way to increase students' vocabulary, enhance fluency, and improve comprehension. As a follow-up activity, we watch *Reading Rainbow*'s version of *The Wall*. I discuss how the father in the story traced his father's name from *The Wall* and demonstrated it by using a sheet of paper, a crayon, and a piece of cardboard with an imprinted name.

Days before the lesson, I search the Internet for names listed on the Vietnam Memorial Wall. Then students make crayon rubbings. They begin with writing the soldier's name on a cardboard template (8" × 3") and trace the letters with school glue. This serves as an imprint and they use peeled crayons and a blank sheet of paper to make their creations. Students enjoy the activity and are proud to display their work on a bulletin board in the hall.

Helpful Tips

- After completing the KWL chart and reading the book, use a large map of the continents and have the students identify North America and Asia.
- After the entire activity, have students watch the *Reading Rainbow* version of *The Wall*. Students will hear the book read again and gain insight on the making of *The Wall*.

CHAPTER 12

To Read or Not to Read

Shakespeare With Fourth Graders

Jacquylynn Brickman

Minneapolis, Minnesota

> *"Our doubts are traitors, and make us lose the good we oft might win, by fearing to attempt."*
>
> —*William Shakespeare's* Measure for Measure *(Act I, Scene IV)*

"I *hate* reading!" yelled Desirée, a fourth grader in my inner-city classroom. I was surprised by this comment, because Desirée was such a mild-mannered young lady and I never heard her yell before. However, I was well aware that students often declare they *hate* something for a variety of reasons. I pulled her aside and sat down next to her on the floor.

Desirée why would you say that?" I whispered. "I thought you liked reading."

"Reading is boring. I mean, my reading teacher is really nice, but I wish I could stay here with you. I go to reading class and all we do is those same stupid workbooks."

That is when my heart sank. Desirée had come to believe that participating in a lesson from a scripted decoding program void of any higher-level questioning was *reading*. Why wouldn't she? Our school even called that time "Collaborative Reading." A team of teachers concentrated on one grade level at a time and pulled all of the below-grade-level readers, as determined by standardized testing, out of the classroom to receive instruction in fluency or decoding for a fifty-minute period each day. The students who were achieving at or above grade level were left with the classroom teacher where they were instructed further through our district basal curriculum. Philosophically, I didn't believe in our "collaborative" model. In addition to the lack of collaboration, I didn't feel that the instruction matched the students' needs. When I questioned the administration about the reading program, they cited numerous examples of other high-poverty, inner-city schools that were adopting similar programs. When I questioned the amount of time my students were taken out of my room, I was told, "It is only fifty minutes out of your day." But fifty minutes can seem like a lifetime to a struggling, disengaged reader and to a teacher who has more content to teach than there are student contact hours in the day. I knew there had to be a better way, a model where the instructional grouping was flexible and based on a variety of data rather than on a standardized test score alone. However, as a second-year teacher, I hadn't yet found my profes-sional voice, the voice that could not only question policy and status quo but also make changes. Veteran teachers in the building advised me to close my door and teach.

As I look back, I am not sure why I felt so passionate about teaching Shakespeare and so sure that it would change my students' attitudes about reading. I do believe that it had something to do with my own intro-duction to Shakespeare, which was required reading at my high school. I had approached my first Shakespeare class with excitement. However, after reading my first Shakespeare play, *Romeo and Juliet,* I was not only disappointed but also confused. I didn't understand what I had read, and, in fact, I felt much like Desirée . . . *I hated it.* Perhaps it was the challenge it posed: taking literature that I hadn't enjoyed reading myself when I was in high school and making it meaningful and motivating to fourth graders. Perhaps it was my attempt at scaffolding this literature for my students, from a very early age. I thought that if they could have some background in Shakespeare now, and *enjoy* it, they be even further motivated in high school and gain an even deeper understanding of the work. What I know for sure is that I saw teaching Shakespeare in elementary school as a way to give my young learners a leg up.

I located a collection of Shakespeare's plays that were rewritten for children (*Shakespeare in the Classroom: Plays for Intermediate Grades* by Dr. Albert Cullum). That book was the missing piece of my puzzle. The major plot elements were left intact, it was written in play form, and it was filled with poetic verse. I was overjoyed. I spent that evening revamping my lesson plans for the following day. I could not wait to begin. I wanted to start this unit off with drama right from the start. As we finished our morning meeting, I explained to the children that I had someone that I wanted them to meet. I stepped into the hall and put on a costume. I came back into the room and introduced myself as Prince Hamlet of Denmark. As Hamlet, I introduced the story to them in order to pique their interest. As soon as I was finished, the students were all leaning forward with looks of anticipation across their faces. They were so excited that they immediately started firing questions at me as if I were Hamlet.

"You mean your mother married your uncle?" shouted one child.

Another yelled, "That is terrible. What are you going to do?"

They also had advice to give him. "You should take care of your uncle! That just ain't right! I bet he killed your father so he could become the king!" Each child thought they knew exactly what Hamlet should do.

I paused and took in the moment. As I laid the playbooks out onto the floor, they actually lunged for them. These were no longer students who *hated* reading, but students who counted the minutes until it was time to read Shakespeare and students who would bring their playbooks to lunch in order to replay some of their favorite lines. Although my students were already part of a strong classroom community, their study of Shakespeare made them an even closer-knit group. Shakespeare had become a kind of secret language among my students, as they made sophisticated jokes in reference to the plays that other classes didn't understand.

Throughout the next few years, I taught a variety of Shakespeare's plays, incorporating many written responses to the text, and eventually each year culminated with a Shakespeare Festival during which my students performed Shakespeare for the other elementary students. The students' favorite plays continued to be *Hamlet, The Taming of the Shrew, Romeo and Juliet,* and *Macbeth.* To my great delight, at the end of the year, Desirée's portfolio reflection sheet listed her favorite school activity as reading, and Shakespeare in particular.

> *"This above all: to thine own self be true." —William Shakespeare's* Hamlet *(Act I, Scene III)*

Helpful Tips

Launching the Unit

- William Shakespeare wrote thought-provoking literature that has stood the test of time. Begin the unit by sharing this idea with your students. Include a "visit" from William Shakespeare himself or perhaps his wife, Anne Hathaway, at the start of the unit, and begin each play with a "visit" from a character. The visitor could be the main character or a character with a smaller part, each having a different perspective. During the introduction, give just enough information to build some prior knowledge and motivate the students. This will encourage further inquiry by the students and motivate them to want to find out how the story unfolds.
- Creating an illustrated timeline of William Shakespeare's life is helpful for students in understanding the author's perspective.

Incorporate Media

- Collect and show clips from cartoons, modern movies, and so on that use lines from and/or other allusions to Shakespeare's plays.
- View multiple film versions of the plays and discuss interpretations.
- View appropriate clips from modern films that are adaptations of Shakespeare's plays (e.g., *10 Things I Hate About You*).

Character Mapping

- Keeping all of the characters straight can be a challenge. Create a large character map (reminiscent of a family tree) with graphics to help students remember who is who.

Vocabulary

- Preteach essential vocabulary that cannot be understood through context.
- Use the vocabulary in your everyday language and encourage students to do the same.

Extend Through Writing

- Write letters to characters.
- Create open-ended prompts to which students can respond.

When Doing Reader's Theater

- For scenes, reassign each part so students have an opportunity to read a variety of parts.
- Appropriately match students to parts: count the number of lines for each character for each scene and assign parts accordingly.
- In order to increase whole-class participation, assign the part with the most lines to the whole class. This way, the entire class can read the majority of the lines chorally and this keeps everyone involved and actively responding. Another suggestion is to assign the male part with the most lines in each scene to all the boys so they can respond chorally and the female part with the most lines in the scene to all the girls so they can respond chorally as well.
- Differentiate through the assignment of parts. Even though the level of difficulty might not change with each part, assigning parts this way allows less fluent readers to participate with fewer lines to struggle through.
- Allow students to "pass" on taking a part of their own, but require them to participate in whole-class parts.
- Consider assigning parts the day before, allowing students to bring the scene home to practice for fluent reading.

▧ Reference

Cullum, A. (1995). *Shakespeare in the classroom: Plays for the intermediate grades.* Redding, CA: Fearon Teaching Aids.

CHAPTER 13

Reaching Fifth Graders With Novel Study

Diane Woodford

South Sioux City, Nebraska

C arol charged up to my desk asking enthusiastically if it was acceptable to write about several parts of her book instead of picking one favorite part. Responding to her gusto, I urged her to expand on the main ideas that transported her into another time. She was sucked into the pages of that book and was compelled to share the action. She immediately journaled ferociously about the book she had conquered. Lance was next. Here was a ten-year-old advising his peers that *Escaping the Giant Wave* was a great evening read. Recommendations from one student to another are powerful. Several boys gathered together and in fifth-grade dialect, oblivious to my presence, heralded this novel as a worthy choice. I smiled at their excitement while I watched them share literary critiques.

Was Carol required to read at home? No, but she was strongly encouraged. Was Lance expected to assist others in choosing their next book? No. However, he knew his recommendation would be accepted.

I learned long ago in my thirty-one-year career as an educator that I do not have the power to require anything. My job is to inspire students to achieve. By the time kids reach fifth grade, they have some fairly strong emotions about school subjects, personal strengths, and weaknesses. A huge chunk of each school day is dedicated to their reading instruction. Students are quick to praise or denounce their individual reading abilities. Most of these prevailing attitudes are directly related to prior report cards and assessment results.

Numbering and sorting students happens all the time due to district assessments, state guidelines, and federal mandates. Teachers must meet the requirements to document those required numerical mazes. Real teaching involves motivating a belief that falling into the footsteps of a character who lives in the pages of a novel is a compelling pastime.

My school year begins with a whole-class novel study. We plunge into a classic like *The Mixed Up Files of Mrs. Basil E. Frankweiler* or *Number the Stars.* Through collaborative reading, this community of learners transports their lives to the Metropolitan Museum of Art or an apartment of a Jewish family during World War II. Together we share. Together we imagine. Together we successfully discover another world. The language on the pages holds the attention of an entire classroom as we read. Each child is asked to be involved. For the child who is less confident in the ability to read fluently, that involvement manifests itself in listening, following along, and thinking. Thinking is evident in the zeal expressed about the suspense of the rising action and the predictions of what is expected next. With my fervor to share a great novel, I inspire students to immerse themselves in reading. After one extraordinary novel is completed, most students believe in the power of literature.

Exemplary literature captivates students. In my opinion, reading only short stories encourages children to gravitate to the shortest book on the shelf because they lack the confidence to read lengthy novels. Instead, use literature-based anthologies that excerpt the great children's authors. Lists of top books are readily available. My students get excited by the fact that by the end of a semester, they have completed many of the books on the list and are familiar with the authors. Get your students addicted to authors such as Gary Paulson, Beverly Cleary, Roald Dahl, Lois Lowry, or Jean Craighead George and watch the unstoppable avalanche of readers rumble through your bookshelves.

Read and write, read and write, read and write. This plan sounds simple because it is. Through modeling, students see how to elaborate on the author's ideas. Relationship building precedes students working independently. A safe classroom is free of sarcasm and abounds with acceptance. This acceptance leads students to write their thoughts without fear of criticism. Asking students to expand on an answer gently encourages more in-depth writing over time. Responsive writing engages readers to think about the plots dumped into their minds. Students have answered the simplistic who, what, when, and where questions for too long. Rejuvenate your strategies and supply open-ended starters for true student engagement. Responding can be quick and painless. By using higher-level thinking skills, students read with a different attitude. The upside for students is that there is no wrong answer.

Encourage your students to use the following strategies in their writing:

- Imagine
- What if
- Plan
- Prove
- Justify

The pursuit of comprehension through literature makes sense. Students respond by improving their written language. Students build relationships through collaboration and expand their worlds through vicarious journeys. Responding to reading, building relationships, and expanding ideas incorporate thinking. Through literature, my students achieve these goals with smiles and enthusiasm.

Components

Silent Reading

Each day students engage in a silent, sustained reading time for twenty-five minutes. We call it USA time, which stands for Uninterrupted Silent Activity. During that slot, I conference with individuals, we discuss their story, and I review their writing responses. My approach is to let the students be the experts. Teachers can find an abundance of red, white, and blue items to be used as incentives. Our USA Record Book has three sections: response writings done daily, vocabulary, and sentence building. As students read, they have a pencil in hand to jot down page numbers, words, or ideas. The books read during this free reading time go home every night.

Literature Circles

Literature circles involve groups that choose a novel by topic. It is run like a book club. They start by having one student make a positive statement, the group rules are reviewed, and then each student responds to the group depending on the job assignment for that day. The visualizer is often the favorite, because drawing is a desired task for fifth graders. A paragraph must accompany the drawing. Students take their jobs seriously. Because the literature circles are student centered, the students are highly motivated to complete tasks, share, and meet deadlines for each other.

At-Home Reading Program

We have a strong at-home reading program. Each year a theme is used to motivate and encourage our student readers. By connecting parents and the home to our reading goals, we strengthen our school–home relationships. Captivating Friday-afternoon announcements share our progress through a point system and announce book winners in each classroom. For our Lewis and Clark theme, we had a tepee that traveled around the classrooms with a box of fiction and nonfiction books related to the expedition. Life-size Seaman dogs were given away at the end of the year.

When we read with our friends around the world, we had international college students visit classrooms. During the winter holiday, we experienced traditions from around the world. In our lunchroom, a world mural marked our journey through nine different countries. As we travel through space this year, students celebrate each month with special activities.

Reading with book buddies, alien visitors, and special student astronaut portraits are all part of our climb toward being better readers. A huge space shuttle glides above our heads in the main hallway to remind students about our reading experiences. We have found that when our students read at home, they progress through guided reading levels and raise their Lexile* reading levels consistently throughout the year.

USA Time, Literature Circles, and our At-Home Reading Program are all centered in the fifth grade on reading full novels. Students are encouraged to finish books and share them with oral book reports. The oral reports enhance presentation skills and cause a contagious interest in the books. My design for a successful intermediate reading program involves reaching them through literature. Positive encouragement leads the motivation for my students to want to read successfully.

---

*The Lexile Framework for Reading from MetaMetrics matches reader ability and text difficulty, allowing for individualized monitoring of progress. This scientific approach to reading and text measurement is the result of more than twenty years of ongoing research.

The Lexile Framework is a scientific approach to reading and text measurement. It includes the Lexile measure and the Lexile scale. The Lexile measure is a reading ability or text difficulty score followed by an "L" (e.g., "850L").

The Lexile scale is a developmental scale for reading ranging from 200L for beginning readers to above 1700L for advanced text. All Lexile framework products, tool, and services rely on the Lexile measure and scale to match reader and text. —Ed.

CHAPTER 14

Reading Kinesthetically

Sharon S. Lancaster

Hopkinsville, Kentucky

The first year I began teaching first grade, a veteran teacher in my team told me, "In first grade, reading and math are the most important subjects you will teach. All the others are just icing on the cake." Her words of wisdom have seen me through all of my years teaching first grade.

Teaching reading can be an extremely challenging but a very rewarding job. Sometimes the child is not developmentally ready to read, or there could be a learning disability, or sometimes I just haven't found the right combination of strategies to make the skills click. I have read, studied, and researched learning styles and created lessons using different multiple intelligences.

▧ Writing With Play Dough

Some of my favorite learning strategies are for the kinesthetic learner. I use play dough to teach my children letter recognition, spelling, and vocabulary. I haven't found a child yet who doesn't like to manipulate and work with play dough. After I introduce the weekly words, I pass out the play dough. The children are then told to soften it. Of course, during this time lots of snakes and hot dogs appear along with giggles and "Look what I made!" I ask the children to look at the first word and I choose someone to spell it out loud. The next step is to tell the children to form the word with play dough. Some children may need help making the letters. My students love helping each other! This is also an excellent way to check fine motor skills. The children continue making and saying the letters and words. By using their hands, I tell my students the words travel up their hands and into their brains so they will always remember them. If time permits, I let the children just play with the play dough—a reward for hard work.

Writing With Shaving Cream

Another strategy the children *love* is messy, so be prepared. You might want to have a smock or old shirt for each child to wear over their clothes. I have my students use shaving cream to "write" their words. I do this activity two ways. The first way is to squirt out a blob of shaving cream on their desks and have the students spread it out to make a work area. The second way is to use a pie pan or cookie sheet for a space. (This method makes cleanup much easier.) We review the words and then the children "write" them with their fingers in the shaving cream. (Some students may have allergies, so I use odor-free products for sensitive skin. Students should be told not to put their fingers on their faces or in their eyes because it will burn.) They then "erase" the word and go on to the next word on the list. There are students who don't like this activity because of the feel of the shaving cream or the messiness. After about ten minutes, the shaving cream loses its fluffiness and disappears. The child may need another squirt, or this could be time to end the lesson and wash off the desks. A reward for hard work is a clean desktop and a classroom that smells good!

My students have enjoyed these activities for many years without realizing they have acquired reading skills. As educators, we take for granted that our students know they can read, but oftentimes they don't realize it. It is wonderful to see my students' eyes sparkle when they realize they can read, and that is why I love teaching first grade!

HelpfulTips

- My students enjoy writing rainbow words. Rainbow words are when the students use their crayons or color pencils to write their spelling or vocabulary words.
- I sometimes have older students look for their spelling words in newspapers or magazines.
- My students enjoy a spelling word search that the Student Technology Leadership Program* (STLP) students create for them.
- Students can cut out words from the newspaper or magazines and create sentences, and then have their buddy read them.
- Peer tutoring and buddy reading are also a big help for those struggling readers.
- A great reward for someone who has really struggled with reading (and all the work has paid off) is to have them read to the principal, secretary, or guidance counselor.

---

*The Student Technology Leadership Program (STLP) is a project-based learning program that empowers students in all grade levels to use technology to learn and achieve. It was established in 1994 by the STLP State Advisory Council, which is composed of teachers, students, and community leaders.

Student-designed projects fall into four categories—instructional, community, technical, and entrepreneurial—and are created to help the school and community while also meeting the six STLP goals. Some activities qualify as service-learning projects and provide assistance to charities or other local agencies in need. Other activities can be described as entrepreneurial and illustrate the beginning steps of forming a small business.

The program is open to *all* students in all grade levels in every school (PreK–16) in Kentucky. —Ed.

CHAPTER *15*

Reading and Writing

A Reciprocal Process

Jessica Heidelberg

Indianapolis, Indiana

There are many rich activities that teach students to read. One activity that greatly impacts the development of early literacy skills is writing. By viewing reading and writing as a reciprocal process, I plan daily instruction that is inherently differentiated. Students write at their developmental level, thus I assess if students know, for example, their letters and sounds, if they display one-to-one correspondence, if the student can read back their own writing, and if the oral and written language remains consistent. Once I have a snapshot of the student's skills, planning for whole-group writing lessons and one-on-one conferences can be completed.

Writing Is Phonics

When planning whole-class writing lessons, I provide a lot of time for demonstration or modeling. When I model writing, students have the opportunity to get inside the brain of a good writer. They can see and hear my thinking as I orally stretch or segment a word into phonemes, assigning letters to these sounds, which results in the desired word in print. I then reread the words, phrases, and sentences to ensure that they make sense. Modeling the process of connecting the oral and written language and giving students time to practice their own writing result in the best-differentiated phonics lessons. Students are also highly interested in this authentic process, so I expect a high level of student engagement.

In order to meet my students' individual needs, I create a time and location in my classroom for one-on-one conferences. At the beginning of a conference, I ask for student input to see what direction they might need that day. By having open dialogue, I can see what the writer needs help with and what the writer does well. Students practice reading their own writing during this time as they explain their ideas and illustrations. I also lead them to other texts that might help them further develop their craft. For example, I had a student who loved to write about horses. I directed her to *Howls* by Gail Gibbson so that she might explore different ways to write and illustrate her facts about horses.

Sharing Develops Fluency

It is also important for students to share their writing with their peers. This can occur in a variety of ways. A classroom might have an "author's chair share" where students read their writing to the class one at a time. Students can share their work with a designated writing partner or in small groups called writing teams. There are many benefits to having assigned writing partners beyond sharing. Peers can get together to problem-solve ideas for writing as well as revising and editing their works. A positive reading outcome from the variety of sharing activities is that students practice reading and rereading their pieces, enabling them to become fluent readers.

Genre Study: Fairy Tales

Next, I plan reading and writing lessons focusing on different genres. I do this by allowing a lot of time for reading of a particular form of writing.

For example, if you wanted to create a cookbook of your family's favorite recipes, you would have to have an understanding of how cookbooks are organized. You might browse other cookbooks to see their layouts and organization. Once you were finished reading many other books, you would come up with a plan for how to write your own cookbook. A few drafts would occur before you were ready for publication. This, too, is the same process I want to provide for my students as they learn to write in different genres through reading. The following genre study is one that I taught in my third-grade classroom. The final outcome was to have students write their own fairy tales.

In the beginning, I ask students to read a variety of fairy tales. This instruction occurs during my guided reading time. We read multiple versions of *Little Red Riding Hood, The Three Little Pigs,* and *Cinderella.* (Meanwhile, I was reading fairy tales aloud daily and we made text-to-text connections between the stories. Some of these fairy tales included *The Princess and the Pea, Rumpelstiltskin, The Golden Goose,* and *Rapunzel.*) The purpose of these readings is to figure out how fairy tales are organized. Students identify the story elements; setting, characters, problem/resolution, and change through time. We chart our work for each text and leave the evidence around the room so we can go back and question, if necessary, as our work continues with each story.

It takes us two weeks to cover these stories in depth and truly understand how a fairy tale is written. Since we read through the lens of a writer, transitioning our understandings of fairy tales to our own writing is easier. Next, during a writing mini-lesson, students create a graphic organizer in their own language based on the fairy tales. As expected, it includes the story elements. We focus a great deal of time on the development of the problem and resolution as it impacted characters' actions in their stories. Scaffolding this process is much more valuable than assigning students to write a fairy tale and giving them the graphic organizer for planning. Instead, students develop their own knowledge by analyzing other works. They are able to take their learning and apply it to their own writing. As drafts are completed, much time and several writing mini-lessons focus on revising and editing for publication.

This kind of genre study can be done with any form of writing. Your state standards and students' interests should drive the kinds of genres you study. These could include poetry, memoirs, persuasive writing, or informational writing like reports and procedures.

Helpful Tips

Writing instruction has a powerful impact on the development of readers in our classrooms. I believe that the benefit of reading and writing as a reciprocal process is greater than we understand.

Additional Resources

■ http://www.readwritethink.org/

ReadWriteThink, a partnership between the International Reading Association (IRA), the National Council of Teachers of English (NCTE), and the Verizon Foundation.

■ http://www.nwp.org/

National Writing Project

CHAPTER 16

Reading Beyond the Lines

Students With Autistic Disorders

Amy Edinger

Cherry Hill, New Jersey

O ne of the "aha" moments in my teaching career occurred when I compared my first trip to Times Square with what the reading experiences of children in my classroom with autism spectrum disorders must be like.

I looked up and my heart started racing. My eyes bounced like a ball in a pinball machine. Images flashed before me in a series of brief visual encounters. It was my first trip to Times Square in New York City. The most memorable experience was the physiological responses I encountered as I walked along the street. I certainly remember glancing at a barrage of signs and seeing words. I imagine I read the words, but for some reason I was unable to retrieve the street name. How did

I connect those words and signs in a way that they would become meaningful enough to comprehend what I was reading?

A pulsation of pain right behind my eyes began to emerge. I struggled to organize my thoughts. "Focus," I thought to myself. I briefly shifted my thoughts to how I was going to pay attention and enjoy my experience. My attempts to will myself into the moment were quickly bombarded with a visual agenda I felt I had no control over. My eyes were beckoned by the flashing lights, colors, and shapes. Everything on that street was competing for my attention. Intimidating buildings demonstrated power as they stared down at me from an infinite height. I was small and insignificant. I couldn't take it anymore. I quit looking. I had failed. I quit reading the environment. It took enormous effort to keep my head positioned down toward the ground, my eyes fixed on the pavement.

For these children, could the experience of reading in my classes be their "Times Square"?

Differentiating instruction goes beyond adapting the curriculum. Consider the challenges students may face when their minds are discriminating and storing information. Too much stimuli or input can overload students and affect the learning process. Observe your students' actions and reactions within the environment. Ask them to explain their perceptions and interpretations. Become a student in your own classroom.

Helpful Tips

- Sit at your students' desks and position yourself so you are observing the classroom from their vantage point. Determine if there are glares that could affect the ability for them to see clearly. For example, laminated posters or graphic organizers may be difficult to see depending on their position on the wall and the way the light reflects off the lamination.
- Look at a worksheet on their desk and avert your gaze as the students might be expected to do during a lesson. Take notice of the time it takes for your vision to adjust and reflect on the pacing of your instruction.
- Anticipate possible distractions.

(Continued)

(Continued)

- Some students may see the "negative space," the space surrounding the actual print. Give students a choice of what color print or paper they would like to use for flash cards.
- Read a page from a book without showing the picture. After reading each sentence, have your students draw a picture about that sentence. When the students are finished drawing their pictures, compare and contrast the students' pictures with the picture in the story.
- Have a student locate an object in the classroom without naming the object. Individually or in teams, students must rely on details or clues to locate the object.
- Practice conversation skills during social interactions. Provide students with a topic to discuss and encourage them to use questions to get more information.
- Students may demonstrate difficulty making connections with the text or story. Prior to reading a specific story, create an activity that would allow students to have an experience that would relate to the story. For example, a family of ducks was rescued from the sewer in our courtyard. After observing the ducks in the courtyard, I read stories about ducks. Students demonstrated an ability to make connections by commenting on their personal experiences with the ducks.

CHAPTER 17

Encouraging Biliteracy

Caridad Alonso

Wilmington, Delaware

M ore than forty years ago, my parents fled a communist regime in their native Cuba and made a dash to freedom to the United States as political refugees. My parents came to this country with one small suitcase and a tiny infant. They left their country, their family, and their home. My mother, a teacher as well as a fluent speaker of both English and Spanish, was determined to provide her daughters with a very rich bicultural upbringing. Born and raised in the United States, I embraced the American culture through school, friends, and music yet maintained loyalty to my ethnic roots by speaking Spanish at home as well as by following my parents' Cuban customs and traditions. Inevitably, being immersed in an English-speaking culture and a Spanish-speaking home, I became a fluent speaker of both languages. Given my success in acquiring both languages, I view linguistic diversity as an asset in our classrooms and for society in general.

In the United States, the increase of culturally and linguistically diverse students has been dramatic and is expected to remain so. Currently, Latinos are the fastest-growing immigrant population and the poorest-achieving academic group. The primary issue at hand is how to rapidly get these non-English speakers to become academically successful in English. Luckily, I teach in a school that values building on students' native language as a means to *increasing* literacy skills in English. Understanding how native language instruction is a bridge for the development of English proficiency is crucial to viewing bilingual programs as an asset.

As the Spanish reading specialist at the William C. Lewis Dual Language Elementary School in Wilmington, Delaware, I have found that increasing literacy achievement in my students' native language— Spanish—assists them tremendously in acquiring high levels of literacy achievement in English. Essentially, students are able to cross-transfer language literacy skills from the first language to the second language. Ultimately, by developing my students' native language, I am helping to reduce the risk of reading problems in English. For this reason, I strongly believe that, when and if possible, schools should provide primary language instruction in order to *facilitate* and *accelerate* the acquisition of English. Biliteracy must become a viable and essential component of educational reform with respect to our underachieving Latino population.

As I reflect upon my students and their success in achieving literacy in both English and Spanish, a very special little girl named Jeishka comes to mind. When I first met Jeishka, she was six years old and in first grade. She had recently arrived from Puerto Rico. Jeishka was very eager to learn; however, she had had no prior schooling. Fortunately, as the Spanish reading specialist, I was able to provide Jeishka with an intensive supplemental literacy intervention program to accelerate reading development in her native language. The results of this intervention coupled with a rich-content English- and Spanish-language classroom environment confirmed yet once again the power of primary language instruction as a means to increase academic achievement. Currently, Jeishka is in fifth grade and is reading on grade level in Spanish and is reading close to grade level in English. According to research, individuals who are literate in a first language are more readily able to acquire literacy in a second one (Cummins, 1996). Therefore, conceptual knowledge learned through one language paves the way for knowledge acquisition in the second language.

According to the 2006 *Report of the National Literacy Panel on Language Minority Children and Youth Sponsored by the U.S. Department of Education* by Diane August, instructional programs work when they provide opportunities for English-language learners to develop proficiency in their native language. We as educators, politicians, and policymakers must adopt this view ourselves. We must support programs such as the Dual Language Program Models that build on our students' home languages and cultures. By promoting biliteracy, students will grow to be tomorrow's business leaders, lawmakers, doctors, and educators who understand how to interact competently in a global economy in which speaking, reading, and writing in more than one language is not only a great job advantage but a growing necessity that is essential for our nation's economic viability.

Local or state policies that block or limit the use of primary language instruction are simply not based on the *best* scientific research available. As a bilingual educator, I do not question that learning English is the *main* goal; however, supporting and building the primary language is key in accelerating the second-language acquisition process. Additionally, I do not want my students' native language to be forgotten in the process. Given my success in acquiring two languages, I want my students to have the same opportunity.

In many foreign countries, bilingualism and multilingualism are seen as a means to personal accomplishment and educational and financial success. In the United States, rather than thinking in terms of an "English-only" culture, we should be promoting an "English plus" culture. If we are to survive as a viable competitive country in a twenty-first-century global community, we must view second-language acquisition as an opportunity to prepare our students to grow and interact competently in this increasingly interdependent world. We as educators should embrace cultural and linguistic diversity allowing for *all* students to have the gift of two or more languages. Being bilingual or multilingual is a gift.

Reference

Cummins, J. (1996). *Educational research in bilingual education.* Retrieved June 2, 2008, from http://www.iteachilearn.com/cummins/

PART II

Reading in
Grades 7–12

CHAPTER *18*

Reflective Practice in the Teaching of Adolescent Reading

Karen Morgan Delbridge, PhD

Cheyenne, Wyoming

L earning with adolescents is what makes teaching spectacular. I am always amazed at the energy students bring to class and frequently overcome with an awesome sense of responsibility. If I am going to really teach and ensure learning, I must first be willing to look within myself and be a reflective practitioner. Reflection as a practitioner should be a constant, daily event in our lives. As teachers, we must know and understand why we teach reading the way we do. In order to understand how to teach adolescents, we must not only look within ourselves but learn to listen to sound research and to the students we teach. Alvermann (2006) recommends that we remain open to the possibility that listening to students for guidance in adapting our instruction is both feasible and worthwhile.

84

▧ Reading as a Process

Adolescents already possess knowledge and skills, and they want to participate in literacy practices that are suited to their own lives. I truly believe that literacy is about learning to read the world, so we must assist our students in exploring how to read the world and how to participate in the different situations in their lives. If we are to do that, we must have a sound definition of what reading is and what it looks like for adolescents. Then we need to understand what those different situations are or could be. What is it that we are preparing students for? First we must look at a sound definition of reading. According to the National Council of Teachers of English (NCTE) Commission on Reading (2004),

> Reading is a complex, purposeful, social and cognitive process in which readers simultaneously use their knowledge of spoken and written language, their knowledge of the topic of the text, and their knowledge of their culture to construct meaning. Reading is not a technical skill acquired once and for all in the primary grades, but rather a developmental process. A reader's competence continues to grow through engagement with various types of texts and wide reading for various purposes over a lifetime. (p. 1)

I appreciate that the definition speaks to how reading is not acquired with finality in the primary grades, and how we are exposed to various texts throughout our lives. Whether it is reading the booklet that my healthcare provider has sent me, reading a road map, or reading my automobile manual to figure out how to change the clock on my radio, I am reading for a purpose . . . and sometimes not very well! So if this is my definition of reading, and I truly believe that we are in this constant process of reading, then how do I help students be thoughtful about the texts they read and prepare them to read for various purposes over a lifetime, and what could those purposes be?

My view of the world is constantly changing based upon my experiences in life. One of those experiences happened this summer after I read *The World Is Flat*. Reading that book forced me to be reflective about the literacy demands of the twenty-first century and caused me to question myself about how I am helping students meet those demands in the classroom. Changes are occurring in the world for which my students need to be prepared. One of the quotes that began my journey of reflection says that leading from good to great does not mean coming up with the answers and then motivating everyone to follow your vision. "It means having the humility to grasp the fact that you do not yet understand enough to have the answers and then to ask the questions that will lead to the best possible insights" (Collins, 2001, p. 75). I have been approaching my reflections with many questions in order to get that best possible insight. What does it mean to think deeply about something? What does it mean to truly understand and comprehend? Am I modeling higher levels of questioning that deepen students' understanding? Are my students able to evaluate sources of information, and am I preparing students for jobs that do not yet exist in this global world?

Exposure and Practice

Looking deeply at literacy, I do know that it is situational. For example, the way a student acts in the hallway is going to be different than how she acts in the workplace. Not only do we want our adolescents to read well, but we want them to be able to communicate effectively in different situations. The literacy demands on students also vary from subject to subject in school. We want them to use their knowledge of spoken and written language, their knowledge of the topic of the text, and their knowledge of their culture to construct meaning. Students need to be given opportunities to read diverse texts. We must expose students to various texts and give them ways to express the ideas that they create by performing in different situations. The text can serve as a tool to help students think critically about issues they are faced with on a daily basis. The text can take its reader beyond the confines of her own prior experience and provide her with material and experience from which new ideas can be formulated (Probst, 2004). The texts that we expose students to do matter. When students are given opportunities to discuss these texts, relationships are built among students, and new ideas emerge. While sharing their own experiences, students begin to be more aware of how they are situated in the world outside of school. That discussion of text is crucial, and this engagement is essential to learning.

▧ Metacognition and Lived Experiences

When we are teaching students, it is no surprise that students will be in different places of learning. No matter where they are, we need to teach all our students to be metacognitive thinkers, to think about their own thinking as they read a text. If literacy is culturally framed and defined, and literacy in the twenty-first century is a concern, then adolescents need to be able to identify the meaning of texts and create their own personal interpretations. We need to not only teach adolescents how to infer and evaluate, analyze, weigh, critique, and rewrite texts not just of literary culture but of popular culture and citizenship but also model those processes for them and with them. Adolescent literacy education is the round table where teachers shape identities and citizens, cultures, and communities (Elkins & Luke, 1999). We ultimately want students to be responsible for their own learning, so by showing students how to approach a text with before, during, and after strategies and by releasing that responsibility to them, we will only help build confident readers.

The view of our world looks different for each student. When we are teaching our students how to pull apart text, we must realize that students come from different places, have different backgrounds, and have different experiences. Those experiences are going to constantly change throughout the life of these students. Reading instruction that is effective will help learners make sense of language (NCTE Commission on Reading, 2004). Whatever the text may be, students bring a certain amount of lived experiences to that text, and teachers must find a way to assist students in activating that prior knowledge. They are able to comprehend texts when they use prior knowledge to construct meaning (Beers, 2002; Robb, 2003). Prior knowledge reflects the experiences, conceptual understandings, attitudes, and values that a student brings to a text; thus it is important to find what connections to personal knowledge and experience students are making. Louise Rosenblatt (1982) believed that thought and feeling are legitimate components of literary interpretation. Whether a text is informational or literary, it will demand a response from its reader, building on the meaning that they bring to the learning situation. Making meaning from texts is critical to reading comprehension, and focused discussion about various academic texts can help students learn to read better at the same time that they comprehend and learn more about a specific field (Applebee et al., 2003; NCTE, 2006).

▧ Last Thoughts

Constantly being reflective about how to teach adolescents, learning to listen to sound research, and listening to the students we teach assist us in ensuring that our students are ready for the literacy demands of the twenty-first century. If we give our students diverse texts, help them be metacognitive in their learning, and practice in those different situations, we will build on the lived experiences that our students bring to the classroom. Reading is a process, and so is teaching. Being constantly reflective will refine our practice and allow us to look into the mirror more easily.

HelpfulTips

- Get to know your students and build relationships with them. Find out where they come from and what their interests are.
- Let your students get to know you. Where do you come from and what are some of your interests? Students love it when they feel and know that you are learning with them.
- Build upon the previous experiences of your students and give them opportunities for discussion through various modes of grouping. In addition, do not be afraid to pull from your own experiences to share with students.
- Teach your students how to be metacognitive with various texts by modeling strategy instruction. You could model through think-alouds with various texts, such as adolescent picture books, brochures, and so on. Then gradually release that responsibility by letting your students practice. This discussion for students is crucial to deeper understanding.

▧ References

Alvermann, D. E. (2006, December). Youth in the middle: Our guides to improve literacy instruction? *Voices from the Middle, 14*(2), 7–13.

Applebee, A., Langer, J., Nystrand, M., & Gamoran, A. (2003). Discussion-based approaches to developing understanding: Classroom instruction and student performance in middle and high school English. *American Educational Research Journal, 40*(3), 685–730.

Beers, K. (2002). *When kids can't read: What teachers can do.* Portsmouth, NH: Heinemann.

Collins, J. (2001). *Good to great.* New York: HarperCollins.

Elkins, J., & Luke, A. (1999, November). Redefining adolescent literacies. *Journal of Adolescent and Adult Literacy, 43*(3), 212–215.

National Council of Teachers of English Commission on Reading. (2004, April). *On reading, learning to read, and effective reading instruction: An overview of what we know and how we know it.* Retrieved October 31, 2006, from http://www.ncte.org/about/over/positions/category/read/118620.htm

Probst, R. E. (2004). *Response and analysis.* Portsmouth, NH: Heinemann.

Robb, L. (2003). *Teaching reading in social students, science, and math.* New York: Scholastic.

Rosenblatt, L. (1982). The literary transaction: Evocation and response. From *Theory Into Practice,* Vol. 21(4). Columbus: Ohio State University College of Education.

CHAPTER 19

I Hate Reading!

Maria I. Davis

Cincinnati, Ohio

"**M**s. Davis, I didn't even bother to do my homework. I hate reading."

"I tried, but I couldn't get into it."

"I fell asleep"

"Me too!"

These are typical comments from my eighth graders at the beginning of the year. In this neighborhood school where more than 95 percent of our student body is African American, 89 percent of our student population receives free or reduced-price lunch, and nearly 25 percent of our student population is identified as having special needs, this is still no excuse for my students to not be able to read.

"Well, you are going to have a difficult time participating in the game today if you did not read," I respond.

I proceed to play a reading game that requires my students to recall, infer, evaluate, and apply last night's reading. When the obvious readers have racked up their points, I check their totals and reward the winner.

"Ah man, I should have done my homework," announces a student. "That's right," I reply, "but I can't make you read."

Although I can't make my students read, I sure do try to encourage them. I try to incorporate as many ways to read as possible without their worrying about the reading but, rather, focusing on the outcome.

One such way is to tell my students that next time they are eating a bowl of cereal, which many of them do several times a day, read the box. Look at the pictures and the labels. A lot of my students admit that they eat alone, and I encourage them to use this time to look at the packages, wrappings, and boxes when they are eating. This is a simple way to encourage them to read without thinking about reading

Another strategy I use to promote reading is to assign watching television for homework. "What?!" they exclaim. I further explain that I want them to try to watch a half hour of TV without the volume and read the closed captions. They find this to be a fun yet challenging assignment without realizing that I have asked them to read for a half hour. The following day discussions are really intriguing. They tell about what they watched, and how they were tempted to turn the volume up, but were amused at the same time. Many of them admit that this is a fun homework assignment.

I also use the newspaper to pique their interest in reading. Reading the newspaper is not a task they enjoy; however, when they are asked to re-create a news broadcast in groups of three or four, the assignment has an entirely different meaning. The groups must report on at least one story in the local, national, sports, and weather sections. Each student must read their article, summarizing it in their own words, and then give an oral report. The most exciting part of this assignment is that each group is videotaped, and when all groups have finished, we watch the video as if it were an actual news broadcast. The students use their own props, colorful backgrounds, and other special touches to make their group's report unique.

Although games, TV, and news broadcasts provide a creative spin on language arts, I know that my students must be responsible for other reading assignments that will better prepare them for testing. I use our district's textbook as well as novels, but getting them to read them is more difficult. My first plan of action is to read aloud.

Even at the junior high level, most of them enjoy being able to sit back and just follow along. Once the basic literary elements such as setting, characters, plot, and so on are established, I put them in pairs—usually a strong reader with a challenged reader—to continue the selection or chapter. At this point, all of my students are engaged in the assignment. Finally, for homework, each student must finish the selected pages along with questions, predictions, or other standards that meet the goals of the lesson. The next day the majority of them are prepared. A quick quiz that requires each student to briefly summarize last night's assignment is an easy way to assess completion. Remembering to choose books or short stories that are stimulating or ones that have relevant connections to their lives is an essential element.

One last strategy that has helped my students over the years is to simply get excited about class. There are times when the first five minutes of class seem like an eternity. Between interruptions, students being unprepared, and my still feeling exhausted after yesterday's drama, it is *very* hard to stand before students and appear motivated and energetic. If you have ever had "one of those teaching days," you know exactly what I mean. Instead of dwelling on yesterday's failures and frustration, close your eyes, say a little prayer, and embrace each day, each class, and each student with enthusiasm, optimism, and a smile. I know that this is easier said than done, but a little positive input in our field goes a lot further than any negative output. If you appear to be excited and enthusiastic about reading or any other subject, then they seem to pick up on your "vibe," and at least some of them will be enthused as well. You already know that motivated students are a lot easier to teach them the not-so-motivated ones.

HelpfulTips

- Get to know your students. Choosing interesting materials will be easier.
- Use various reading materials: short stories, poetry, magazines, novels, and so on.

- Start the year with an easy reading selection, even below grade level if necessary. This will engage your challenged readers.
- Use a variety of teaching methods and styles.
- Read to your class with enthusiasm.
- Greet your students each day with a smile.

CHAPTER 20

The "I Hate Reading" Club

Jill Saceman Ryerson

Dalton, Georgia

During my six years as a first-grade teacher, reading was a focus of excitement. Seeing the faces of children light up in an all-consuming smile as reading came into their lives became my inspiration and driving force. While meeting standards, we read and learned about penguins, culminating our unit with a trip to Sea World for a backstage up-close-and-personal visit with these exciting birds. To learn about the first Thanksgiving, we read about it and then held a mock feast on the grounds of our school and dressed as Pilgrims and Indians. We read and learned about other cultures, culminating our lessons by transforming our classroom into a Japanese environment where students taught other classes and parents what they had learned.

Now, as a seventh-grade language arts/reading teacher, I find that the light has dimmed in, if not altogether vanished from, the eyes of my students. Yes, there are a few who are absorbed in books and refuse to put them down; however, most of them have come to view reading as a requirement they hate. "Reading for pleasure" has become an alien concept to these students. How, then, are the youth of today going to be able to make valuable connections and grow to understand themselves and others if not through literature?

My seventh-grade students are in the tumultuous, preadolescent stage during which I believe a love for reading and learning must be taught, modeled, and—all too often—revived. Hence, I started the "I Hate Reading" Club. In it, students who say they hate reading share and discuss the books they have read and enjoyed. I compile a list that is constantly being updated as the reading haters begin to inspire each other with dialogue about books that they are reading and enjoying. It is truly inspirational when a student trudges out the door with a book and a goal and returns the next day screaming with excitement that she finished the book last night because she couldn't put it down. Others gather around as they hear the excitement and inquire about the piece, while offering their own suggestions for a really good read. The room ignites into a firestorm of discussion.

Does this happen to each and every student? No, but helping a few who help a few more who help a few more builds a group that grows exponentially. There is not a day that goes by in which I am not reading to or with students in order to build understanding, not to just check an item off a state reading list. The reading selections in my class are thought-provoking pieces of literature that help students relate to the world around them. Former students ask in passing if we still read *Hatchet* and eat an MRE (meal ready to eat) in class like Brian, the protagonist, had to eat; or if we still read *Nightjohn* in the woods off our nature trail, to try and capture a little of the experience forced upon slaves while running and hiding for their lives. *A Christmas Carol* (unabridged) and *The Autobiography of Malcolm X* are two pieces that we read while listening to Jim Dale and Joe Morton as they bring these texts to life with their expressive voices on an audiobook CD. I do not push "play" and walk away; we pause throughout to analyze and predict text. Students also read aloud, mimicking the fluency and expression of the professionals within their groups. As I rove around the room, I am inspired by their comments and support for each other. Such literature helps them to view the world differently while opening their minds to new ideas.

My goal is to design engaging work and offer creative experiences for my students so that they not only attain mastery of the standards but also develop a love of reading and literature and, better yet, a love of learning. It is not only literature that can be read within this kind of engagement. I currently teach a seventh-grade social studies class where state standards map *what* we teach, but not *how* we teach. Before reading for information, my students determine with my help and guidance what information we will be seeking. I am a facilitator. Research shows that only 10 percent of what is read or heard in a lecture is retained; however, 90 percent of what is discussed and taught is retained. As a facilitator, then, I guide proper discussion and create work for students in the investigation of what seems to many of them boring material. For the last few years, I have been a student of the Schlechty Center for school reform. The Working on the Work (WOW) framework from this center has focused my work around student engagement and the designing of work that is challenging, rigorous, and—most importantly—interesting for my students.

No media outlet can offer experiences, insight, and thinking like reading can. As educators, we must keep the minds of our youth alive and thriving in a world of technological advances. I continue to search for innovations that will help engage my students. My most recent endeavor was to order Kindle* after reading an article in *Newsweek* about the future of reading. My students and I are excited about the advancement in text, and hopefully I am inspiring them to always want to know more no matter what their interests are. That is why I'm here—that is why I teach.

---

*Kindle is a convenient, portable reading device with the ability to wirelessly download books, blogs, magazines, and newspapers and is produced by Amazon. —Ed.

CHAPTER *21*

You Simply
Need to Love It!

Heather-Lee M. Baron

Union City, Pennsylvania

I received a phone call during my third-block reading class. The voice on the other line greeted me and went on to say, "This is Dr. Randi Stone from Corwin Press. . . ." She continued to explain that she was putting together a book for teachers written by teachers about the best practices for teaching reading and that she would like me to contribute to it. Agreeing to look over the materials she would be sending me, I hung up the phone in calm disbelief. I researched Dr. Stone and Corwin Press. Then I thought, "What could *I* possibly contribute to such a book?" I considered writing something scientific, a masterpiece having a profound effect on the profession. I'd be the next Catherine E. Snow or even Lev Vygotsky; maybe as admired and respected as Patricia Cunningham and Dorothy Hall.

I took the remainder of the day to ponder over my curriculum, glance at reference books in my enormous professional library, and ponder the reading strategies I use and firmly believe in. The topics to write on were becoming endless. Finally, on my drive home I asked myself, "Heather, what makes *you* a good reading teacher?" and it hit me. The answer to the question "What could *I* possibly contribute?" was right there in me the whole time . . . I love it! I love teaching reading. It is my passion. *That* is what truly makes me a good reading teacher, and I believe it is the same thing that makes all good teachers just that, good teachers. The answer was that obvious.

You can teach solid research-based strategies, attend conference after conference, take numerous classes on how best to teach your students, and read all of the literature out there, but nothing will help your readers more than your own enthusiasm—your own desire to help them become readers and to read better. It is like a disease that attacks the mind. The fervor is contagious and infectious. As a reading teacher, you must be passionate about what you do and understand in your core being and believe in your heart just how important reading is. You must fully understand that through reading, you can open up the whole world to your students. Through reading, they can accomplish anything, learn everything, and go anywhere.

Thus, the best practice for teaching reading is to love what you do!

Helpful Tips

Enjoy the students you teach!

- Get to know your students.
- Learn each student's reading abilities.
- Get a book into each student's hand that you know they will take pleasure in and be capable of reading.

Enjoy reading yourself!

- Read, read, read and tell your students about it.
- Don't be afraid to read books at your students' reading levels.
- Share the books, magazines, articles, journals, and newspapers that you read with your students and suggest that they read some.
- Show them how you read these items, and model the strategies you used to help you better understand them.

- Be honest. Tell them if you liked something, but don't be afraid to tell them if you didn't.

Enjoy learning!

- Keep current. Take classes and continue to grow professionally.
- Tell your students about your classes.
- Make connections between what you are learning, what you are teaching, and how best you can adapt all of it to each individual child.

CHAPTER 22

Digging Deeper for Comprehension

Jessica Galla

Lincoln, Rhode Island

People are often shocked when I tell them I'm a high school reading specialist. They believe that students at the secondary level shouldn't or don't have reading problems. Well, many secondary students *do* have reading issues. At this point, they are in high school and have trouble reading, which means they can't understand many things that go on in the classroom. They become frustrated and sometimes that means they become behavior problems.

There are many things to do to help the struggling reader in your classroom. It is not as simple as telling the student to try harder. A student reading on a seventh-grade level could be in a ninth-grade physics class, using a textbook written on a tenth-grade level; in such a situation, his best effort just may not be enough. It is our job, as educators, to help; all teachers, not just English teachers, should teach their students strategies to become successful in the classroom.

There are seven proficient reading strategies that I find very helpful to use: (1) asking questions, (2) making predictions, (3) making connections, (4) visualizing, (5) determining important information, (6) synthesizing, and (7) making inferences. Of these, I believe the three most difficult reading strategies to understand are determining what information is important, synthesizing all the information, and making inferences. Synthesizing information is hard for students to understand at first. A puzzle usually helps with this. If you give each student a piece of a puzzle and ask them to tell you about the whole puzzle, it is difficult for them to do that. If they work together to make the puzzle, they can see the whole picture. Synthesizing is like solving the puzzle: You use what you already know, and you add new pieces of information you take in along the way. You add all the important information together. Students make inferences every day without using the term *inference*. This is when the author doesn't specifically state something but you can read between the lines to figure it out.

Using prereading, during-reading, and postreading strategies when you teach will also help your students achieve. There are many strategies that could fall under these three categories; I am going to explain a few. Many struggling readers don't know why they are reading or how to activate their background knowledge about the subject before they read. These strategies help them to do that. Front-loading critical vocabulary is key. Preview the important vocabulary before you read. This will allow students to activate their background knowledge on the subject. Less is more with vocabulary words. Don't pick twenty important words for the students to know. That will overwhelm them, and studies have shown that students will be more likely to retain the words when there are six or seven.

Word Splash is also another great prereading activity. Word Splash allows students to activate their prior knowledge and discuss key vocabulary terms all at once. Choose six or seven words that you believe are important in your text. Post them on the board or make copies of them for your students. Have your students make predictions on how the words may connect to each other and what the text may be about. Then have your students write a paragraph on the board about their predictions using the six or seven words. Students should either work in pairs to discuss their predictions or do this with the whole group. When students are sharing their predictions, it allows other students to gain more knowledge. After sharing, the students should read the text, then go back to their original paragraph and change or tweak the information. This activity allows students to activate their prior knowledge while focusing on the key vocabulary for the lesson.

Reciprocal teaching is a wonderful strategy for improving comprehension. The four components of this strategy are predicting, questioning, clarifying, and summarizing. Pair up the students and have them read the assigned text. You can break the text up into sections; it may be a paragraph at a time at the beginning. One student will read the text aloud and stop as directed. The other student's job will be to summarize what was just read. They both could clarify. Sometimes a student may not know what a word means or may be confused by something. By speaking with another student, such questions can often be resolved. The students can then form questions and make predictions on the next part that they would be reading. This strategy allows students to be interactive while reading. When it's successful, the students take ownership of their learning.

Another successful strategy is Save the Last Word for Me. This strategy can be used during and after reading. The students are in groups of about five, and they are each given five index cards. While or after the students read the selected text, they write down five statements that they find interesting, are confused about, or disagree with. The students then write their reactions to the statement on the back of the card. After all the students write down five statements and reactions, one person reads their statement to the group. After that student reads their card to the group, they turn it around so the group can read it to themselves. The person to the right of them tells their group their reaction to the statement. Each member of the group does the same. The person who read their statement now shares their reaction. (That is why the strategy is called Save the Last Word for Me.) After each member of the group has a turn to share their cards, each group can share with the whole class one statement their group found interesting. This strategy allows for deeper understanding of the text. Each member is pulling out important information from the text and sharing with the group, which allows students to interact with each other as well as with the text. There are many prereading, during-reading, and postreading strategies. I tried to pick practical ones that you could do tomorrow. Enjoy.

Helpful Tips

- Find audiotaped versions of required text.
- Teach the students practical strategies that could be used in any subject.
- Model, model, model. It will take time. Give the strategy time to work.
- Have fun with your students.

CHAPTER 23

Using Wonder Journals to Teach Research Reading and Writing Skills

Jill Dougherty

Springfield, Pennsylvania

O ne strategy that has been particularly successful with both students and their teachers is student journals. In my class, we have used journaling to respond to self-selected independent reading books or to provide a place for students to record what they are thinking as we activate their prior knowledge. It wasn't until I used Wonder Journals with my reading enrichment groups that I discovered a structured way for my students to respond to informational reading in a format that also teaches skills needed in research writing. Wonder Journals reinforce the skills that help students read informational text and respond to higher-order questions that increase understanding.

Through my role as literacy specialist, I support the students in all content areas in a variety of capacities. I teach small groups of reading enrichment that help ninth-grade struggling readers learn the strategies they need to become proficient readers across all content areas. I also provide in-class support to the ninth-grade students through coteaching or by providing model lessons that apply strategic reading to classroom learning. Another aspect of my position is to create and deliver monthly professional development ideas to assist teachers in implementing strategic reading in their lessons.

Wonder Journals take advantage of the high computer–student ratio we have at Springfield High School, thanks to the Pennsylvania Classrooms of the Future Grant. The focus of the activity is to provide students with many opportunities to receive instruction and practice the wide range of skills that they must master to be successful research readers and writers. The reading enrichment students in my class who successfully participated in the activity reported that they were better able to complete research papers in their language arts and social studies classes.

⬚ What Are Wonder Journals?

Wonder Journals comprise a multistep journaling strategy that, once taught through direct instruction, can be applied across the curriculum to provide a record of a student's research reading and writing. The steps for journaling are as follows:

- Students must ask an in-depth question that is connected to the content. The question should extend beyond what the student is learning in class and should focus on something that the individual student would like to learn more about.
- After recording the question in their journal, the student then researches the answer to their question using online resources that may include GaleNet, Power Library, and Groves Art. Students also have the option to use other Web sites, if they are able to prove the site's reliability.

- After reading the information they find, students answer their questions using an open response strategy, and they document their source using a Modern Language Association (MLA) citation.
- The completed entry is saved in the student's Wonder Journal.

Where Can Wonder Journals Be Stored?

Originally, my students kept their Wonder Journals as traditional spiral-bound notebooks; as the technology available in my classroom has increased (and therefore my comfort level), students now store their journals electronically. We are currently using Moodle, a course management system that allows students to post their entries for the entire class to view. Because my students know that their peers will be able to see their work, they are writing more carefully. Moodle is a free service, but it does require district servers to access it, and there are other related costs for technology support. I am able to grade the students' work online and eliminate some of the paper generated in my class. Moodle also gives students the ability to edit their work after receiving feedback from myself or their peers. The next level to which I would take Wonder Journals would be a message board, where I hope to have students respond to and build on each other's entries and become a true community of investigators.

Why Wonder Journals Now?

The role of questioning has changed in the twenty-first-century classroom; students are no longer being asked to read the textbook and answer the questions at the end of the chapter. They are now becoming consumers of a vast amount of available information. Students often feel overwhelmed just choosing what they should read. Self-questioning techniques are being taught to help students monitor the text they are reading. This technique helps students focus on a purpose for reading and provides a framework for comprehension.

Much of the literature today stresses the importance of teachers participating in the journaling process. Teachers can model the power of questions by using real-life examples from their own world. In my own class, I asked about the safety of the product Splenda® and researched what the scientists thought about the sugar substitute. Other possible topics may include the best new car, how to prepare a Thanksgiving turkey, or what is the proper way to refinish a hardwood floor. Regardless of a student's future career choice, all citizens must be able to wade through information both online and in traditional print and make life decisions based on what they glean from the sources they choose. Some of the critical reading skills that will prepare them for this include determining the reliability of a source, identifying an author's bias, paraphrasing information read, and giving proper credit to a source when using the information. I refer to my own questions to illustrate each of these skills. Many of my students are amazed at the amount of reading I do outside of school. "You mean you read when you are not teaching reading?" is one of my favorite lines from a student.

Wonder Journal Procedures

Students are taught the questioning strategy using a Big Mac versus the cheeseburger metaphor and are then asked to participate in an interview activity. I use this fast-food metaphor to help students see the two different types of questions. Cheeseburger questions ask for a small detail. This kind of question is good when you need a small amount of information to satisfy your appetite. The Big Mac question is for when you are really hungry for a lot of information. If you ask a bigger question, you get a bigger answer. Two groups of students are asked to create interview questions to write an article about me for the school newspaper. The first group of students is asked to create six cheeseburger questions for an interview, and the second group is asked to create three Big Mac questions. The groups ask the questions when the class comes back to one large group. I answer the questions, and the students are asked to take notes as fast as they can. Because they are not responsible for writing the article, I answer as fast as I can and try to provide them with as much information as I can. Students quickly see the amount of information they access with the right kind of question. The class debriefs on which type of questioning leads to good information answers. Students then practice creating questions to glean information they are curious about. Because reading skills are my curriculum, students are able to freely choose topics to wonder about. Here are some of my examples from my students:

- Why does X stand for a kiss and O stand for a hug?
- Why do so many teenagers run away from home?
- How many branches of the military are there and what are they?
- What is the smallest breed of dog in the world?
- Is Terrell Owens going to be healthy for the playoffs?
- Why do we have to learn about evolution in school if everybody has their own opinion?
- Bipolar disorder—what is it and how does it affect us?
- Why is smoking dangerous?

After the questioning activity, students are taught how to use the online resources available on the laptop computers. The librarian gives the students a virtual tour of the resources. The students then complete an activity where they answer one of their wonder questions using one of the sources just presented. At this point, they are given instructions on using the Citation Machine Web site to cite their sources using the MLA format, which will be required for all Wonder Journal entries. Because students also have the option of using Web sites they find using search engines, they are taught how to determine author reliability and author bias in future mini-lessons.

The next mini-lesson will teach students to use the RACE strategy to answer their questions. RACE is an acronym that stands for

- **Restate** the prompt
- **Answer** all parts of the prompt
- **Cite** information from the text
- **Edit** for spelling and grammar

Posters explaining the strategy are posted in each room, and students practice this type of written response to encourage complete answers that will score a 3 in state testing. It is my hope that repeated practice answering questions using the RACE strategy will help students provide complete answers on the PSSA open-ended reading prompt and positively impact their reading scores.

Here is an example of one student's early Wonder Journal entries:

"Why does X stand for a kiss? and O stand for hug?"

"Why do we write X for kisses and O's for hugs? We write X for kisses and O's for hugs because people couldn't read and write long ago. So they would write X instead of signing their name. They signed an X to represent the cross of St. Andrews or the bible. They also kissed the X to show good faith. and they say that the reason O means hugs is because of the shape of your arms when you hug somebody."

This is not the student's first edit. After he first posted the entry, he and I were able to conference and discuss using good paraphrasing skills. After the conference, the student rewrote his entry including the same information using his own words. The student was excited to see that he was able to produce original work after the conference.

As the semester progresses, I have a record of the students' progress in the following areas:

- Open-ended response writing
- Creating in-depth questions
- Paraphrasing
- Finding appropriate reliable sources
- Identifying the author's bias
- Using the MLA format for writing
- Using online resources
- Reading for content information

Wonder Journals are a cross-curricular journaling technique that provides the scaffolding that students need to be successful reading independently in their classes. This strategy will both support struggling readers and help good readers dig deeper for information that makes them curious. This strategy would naturally lead to student presentation opportunities, allowing students to be the expert on the material they research. Students who are given repeated exposure to the skills focused on in Wonder Journals will more become confident in all areas of content-area reading and research writing. Wonder Journals require a significant amount of preteaching skills and a commitment from the teacher to provide time to journal in class. It will, however, engage and impact learners of all abilities.

HelpfulTips

- Once you teach questioning, have your students brainstorm lists of questions that they store in their journal. They can refer to these questions on days when they feel less inspired.
- Phase in the journal slowly. Teach each skill independently, and provide them time to practice the skill before you add new skills.
- Use online resources for writing citations such as www.citation machine.net. It is quicker and allows you to spend the time teach ing them why citing sources is important.
- Encourage kids to "wonder" across their content-area classes, and show them how they can take small wonders and turn them into larger, more formal research projects.
- Wonder along with your students, and encourage other teachers and administrators to submit their own entries; they make great models for the students and helps kids connect to the larger school community.

▧ Helpful Resources

Biancarosa, G., & Snow, C. E. (2004). *Reading next—A vision for action and research in middle and high school literacy: A report to Carnegie Corporation of New York.* Washington, DC: Alliance for Excellent Education.

Gallagher, K. (2004). *Deeper reading.* Portland, ME: Stenhouse.

Harvey, S. (1998). *Nonfiction matters: Reading, writing and researching in Grades 3–8.* York, ME: Stenhouse.

Harvey, S, & Goudvis, A. (2007). *Strategies that work* (2nd ed.). Portland, ME: Stenhouse.

Kooy, M., & Wells, J. (1996). *Reading response logs: Inviting students to explore novels, short stories, plays, poetry and more.* Portsmouth, NH: Heinemann.

Tovani, C. (2000). *I read it, but I don't get it.* Portland, ME: Stenhouse.

CHAPTER 24

Make It Your Own!

A Vocabulary Activity

Heather-Lee M. Baron

Union City, Pennsylvania

Vocabulary is the foundation necessary for strong literacy skills. Research has proven time and again that vocabulary is critical for reading success. Literacy skills and the construction of an extensive vocabulary begin before birth and continue throughout an entire lifetime. The more words a student has in his mental lexicon, the more words he will be able to recognize as he reads. This will aid in reading fluency and in turn help with comprehension.

Several groundbreaking studies have proven that a great deal of language learning occurs within the first three years of life. Luckily, humans appear to be "prewired" to teach language. When talking to small children, a mother often uses "baby talk." Her speech becomes shorter, choppier; easier, and she speaks to her child in high-pitched, rhythmic intonations, accentuating the vowel sounds. This phenomenon has been coined "motherese," and it appears to be one of the first steps in language teaching and learning.

However, teachers do not have access to children while they are still in the womb, and most do not work with them until they are five or six years old. But with the growing popularity of preschool, some children are being taught language skills at three or four years of age. There are many vocabulary teaching strategies and techniques, and teachers can help their students improve their vocabulary at any age and/or grade level.

▨ Make It Your Own!

An activity I use to teach vocabulary in my classes is what we refer to as Make It Your Own! Because a person needs to use a word appropriately roughly ten times before they have truly mastered it, Make It Your Own! really gets the students using and thinking about their vocabulary words.

It is very important to make sure that all the vocabulary words that are taught are relevant to what the students are learning in their classes at the time. This will ensure that they not only hear and use the words during this activity, they will also hear and use them on other occasions. It will also allow opportunities for the students to make connections between the words and what they are learning.

- OBJECTIVE: The objective of this activity is to ultimately learn the vocabulary for the upcoming lesson. The activity will also add to the students' mental lexicons.
- OUTCOME: Each group of students will have a PowerPoint presentation using all of their vocabulary words.
- TIME: Fifty minutes for a list of ten words.
- REQUIREMENTS: Each PowerPoint slide must contain:
    o The vocabulary word.
    o The article of speech the word is an example of.
    o The word's definition summarized using the students' own words.
    o A picture/graphic depicting the word's meaning.
    o A sentence explaining what the word reminds them of. The sentence must contain the word itself.

- LESSON:
  - o Students work in groups of five (or any number that best fits the class at hand).
  - o Each group will brainstorm what they would like to place on each slide, creating a brief outline.
  - o Once their outline has been approved by the teacher, they will then create their PowerPoint presentation meeting the above requirements.
  - o Each presentation will then be transferred to the teacher's computer for evaluation.

- ADDITIONAL ACTIVITIES (time permitting):
  - o Each student produces his or her own PowerPoint presentation.
  - o Each group may give their presentation pronouncing the word, explaining its definition and how the definition affects the article of speech the word represents, why they chose the picture they did, and what the word reminds each student of.
  - o The teacher may select one or two slides from each group and create a class PowerPoint presentation, then present the PowerPoint to the class explaining why each slide was selected.
  - o The teacher may select one or two slides from each group and create a class PowerPoint presentation. Then as each group's slide(s) appears, they may pronounce the word, explain its definition and how the definition affects the article of speech the word represents, why they chose the picture they did, and what the word reminds them of.

Now They Own It!

This simple activity requires the students to use the word appropriately various times, approaching the goal of ten times or more! More importantly, this activity not only allows the students to use the word, but they must think about the word. This helps the students connect the vocabulary word and its meaning to their own prior knowledge, in turn aiding in their long-term memory. Now they own it!

Oxymoron
Little Giant

Summarized definition: A set of words or a phrase that is contradictory.

Part of speech: Either adjective and noun or adverb and adjective.

This word reminds me of: The picture we used for the word **oxymoron** reminds us of the cover of Jonathon Swift's *Gulliver's Travels*.

Helpful Tips

- Begin the activity before starting the lesson in which the words are used.
- Make the vocabulary words relevant to what you are teaching.
- Have your students use the words appropriately multiple times.
- Have your students use the words in various contexts.
- Have your students make personal connections to each word.
- Have your students make the words their own!

CHAPTER 25

Teaching Reading in the Math Classroom

Greg Andersen

Colorado Springs, Colorado

Math teachers across the country are constantly challenged by the cliché, "All teachers are reading teachers." Much like the students sitting in math classrooms, math teachers often wonder, "Why do I have to do this?" as if teaching math alone isn't challenging enough already. However, upon closer examination, students develop and construct math concepts much the same way they learn to read. They do this by putting letters, numbers, and symbols in a meaningful order to understand and communicate ideas, concepts, and answers. In fact, the objectives of developing good readers are much the same as developing good math students. Teaching reading in math will help students extract meaning from data and develop verbal reasoning and logic skills that will allow them to arrive at a conclusion following a series of steps. Reading in the math classroom will also help students recognize and explain patterns and communicate math thoughts, concepts, and processes.

Math teachers face many challenges to teaching reading to their students. One challenge is that math books don't read like novels. Students looking for action or a climax to the story are often left unfulfilled. Another challenge is that learning math is an active process. Mastering math concepts requires picking up a pencil, practicing, correcting, reworking, and reflecting. Math is not a spectator sport. Finally, many math courses have a full curriculum that must be completed in a timely manner in order to prepare their students for the next level of math, state tests, and college entrance exams. Who has time to teach reading? However, teaching reading in the math classroom facilitates a deeper understanding of the concepts as well as helps the student take responsibility for their learning. Teaching reading is teaching math.

It's easy to assume that students struggling in math class have math problems when, in fact, some of these students may have reading problems. Teaching reading in the math classroom will not only facilitate students' learning of math concepts but will help students develop the confidence to succeed in all classes. Teaching reading in the math classroom using a consistent and systematic approach will aid students in reflecting and taking responsibility for their learning. Only then will we give students the necessary daily living skills that allow them to make meaningful use of math after their classroom days are done.

Helpful Tips

- Invest time in getting to know the reading levels of your students. Reluctant learners in the math classroom may have reading problems that have been diagnosed by previous teachers. Take advantage of school resource specialists and parents, and, most of all, talk to the student. These students will most likely struggle with confidence issues despite being capable math students.
- Determine the reading level of your text. Is it age and ability appropriate?
- Preread assigned reading with students. Many math textbooks will highlight important vocabulary and concepts with colored boxes,

---

(Continued)

(Continued)

boldface print, and italics. This is also a great time to model reading strategies for students by verbally discussing how to read for meaning.

■ Have sticky notes available for students to write down questions or thoughts as they read through a section.

■ Build a mini-library of different textbooks that explain concepts at different levels. The library should include a math dictionary.

■ Have students engage in partner reading. This will allow students to summarize and share their understanding of the reading as well as appeal to the interpersonal learners that fill our classrooms.

■ Provide prompts such as worksheets that will help math readers focus on reading for meaning and develop personal strategies for reading math books.

■ Give relevant assignments such as having students read articles, and then have them use and organize the data in a persuasive argument. This will allow students to connect the reading and the math concepts to their everyday lives.

CHAPTER 26

Reading the Language of Mathematics

Anita Tortorici Dobbs

Trussville, Alabama

Reading is essential within the mathematics classroom. Students in middle school feel that math problems should involve only numbers. However, students need to understand the importance of word problems and how to read these problems for meaning. It doesn't matter how well a student can compute if he cannot make sense of what the problem is asking. Often real-world problems for mathematics are not straightforward and require multiple steps, especially problems involving decimals and percents. Working through these steps involves critical reading. I have asked my students, when reading a problem, to underline key words to help find the solution. This helps reinforce reading for meaning and learning the vocabulary of mathematics.

Students have fewer difficulties solving mathematical problems when they read and understand the vocabulary. I remind students constantly to "speak math." They need to be able to describe mathematical procedures not only with numbers but also with words. Therefore, I have incorporated more word problems in which students demonstrate the mathematical procedure and describe the steps in words. Since many students are verbally oriented, this approach affords these students opportunities to express themselves mathematically. A student's understanding is especially easy to assess when they use mathematical vocabulary. For example, when students use the word *numerator* instead of *top number* for fractions, I can see quickly that they have grasped the concept and will be able to read word problems correctly. Working math problems both procedurally and verbally helps students speak mathematically; therefore, they read mathematically.

One way I emphasize the importance of reading in the mathematics class is through research. I have been fortunate to have access to wireless Internet for my students. Every year, groups use the Internet in order to participate in a stock market simulation. The students have "$100,000" to invest in the stock market. They "buy" and "sell" stocks based on research they have done. Reading is essential for students to be able to make wise investments. Our school receives a classroom set of the local newspaper every day, and the students use this source to stay current with events that will affect the stock market. I have found through the years that by participating in the simulation, students are much more motivated to do the research and the reading, since they can clearly see its real-world application.

Reading in mathematics cannot be taken lightly. Students do not always see that there is a connection between the two. Our job is to have students see how subjects are interrelated and to impress upon them the importance of reading for meaning. When they see these connections, they will be able to strengthen their vocabulary to communicate, to speak, and to read mathematically.

Helpful Tips

- Always have students use correct mathematical terms.
- Use word problems that simulate real-world problems.
- Have students read and interpret different approaches to the same mathematical problem, using research appropriate to the age level of the student.

- Have students underline key words when they read math problems.
- Allow students to explain their problems verbally so that they can communicate mathematically.
- Encourage students to take time to read a math problem more than once.
- Allow cooperative learning so that students communicate with peers.
- Make mathematics interesting enough that students want to read and research more independently.

CHAPTER 27

"Who in the World Are You?"

An Interdisciplinary Project

Janet K. Vaine

Jacksonville, Florida

How many times have you heard the rumble of discontent when you announce to your class that they are going to participate in a research project? Sometimes the force of "argh" can literally knock you off your feet. Don't you wish there was a great idea out there to encourage students to conduct research willingly and not hear the words we as teachers hear far too often like, "Why do I have to do this?" or "I hate research!"? Wouldn't it be a welcome change to announce a research project and hear, "Oh yeah!"?

"Who in the World Are You?" encourages students to want to participate in research by making the research relevant. It keeps students engaged because the topic is one to which they can really connect, encourages parental involvement because the topic includes not only the child but also their parents, and promotes lifelong learning and allows them to tap into the creative side of their thinking to create a keepsake that is certain to become a family heirloom.

Giving "tweens" and teens a topic they'll love will encourage the research process to take place easily. What topic could be better for these adolescents than themselves? Toby Keith certainly pegs our middle school students accurately when he sings, "I wanna talk about number one, oh my, me my. . . ." Not only does this research unit allow them to talk about themselves, it allows them to see the "why" behind conducting research. The information connects directly to their lives by investigating and discovering their own family's history.

In today's classroom, no project or unit is worth investing time and effort planning unless it fits your district's curriculum and standards. Spending time and effort planning innovative lessons and projects that directly link to your curriculum and standards can be tedious. My "Who in the World Are You?" research unit was developed as an attempt to tackle all of those important tasks teachers face: encouraging middle school students to want to conduct research while connecting to the sixth-grade curriculum and the language arts standards. Since I teach both language arts and social studies, I developed this interdisciplinary unit that would accomplish all those goals. The social studies curriculum encompassed the rich cultures that span our globe, from the culture of prehistoric nomads to that of modern societies. My students were expected to learn how culture shapes and defines a group of people. What better culture and history to study than your own?

For those of us who teach in the middle school arena, cross-curricular projects are viewed as worthy endeavors because they allow our students to see how what they learn in one class links to what they learn in another class. Offering one project for two classes is also an attractive offer for middle schoolers. Since I taught the same group of sixth graders twice a day, developing a project that would meet the demands of our social studies curriculum and help students meet the language arts standards was an advantageous plan. "Who in the World Are You?"

links the study of cultures to their own families while applying information learned and practiced in language arts. Studying culture was now relevant and made sense to them. Likewise, research was now relevant, enabling my students to make connections to the information. Furthermore, reading and writing had a specific and relevant purpose. My students could see "why" they had to involve the reluctant readers and writers who wanted to participate in this project.

Like many grandparents, my grandma told and retold family stories as my sisters and I grew up. As grandmas tend to be, she was always somewhat worried that we wouldn't remember the family stories so that we could pass them on to our children when she was gone. My grandma, Granny Winnie, began participating in genealogy during the 1970s, spending hours upon hours researching family history. She took great pride compiling information she gathered into albums to share with my sisters and me. To this experience, I credit my own scrapbooking. I have not been compiling pictures and other family artifacts for long, but the albums I have created so far have already become priceless heirlooms my children enjoy flipping through over and over. As those of you who teach middle school students can attest, instilling a sense of accomplishment and pride in adolescents while cleverly sneaking in the curriculum and standards is a feat that brings numerous rewards.

You're probably thinking that this all sounds well and good, but how do I get started? This project does take a bit of preliminary work to make it successful. As an anticipatory strategy and to get my students fired up about the project, a week or so before we begin the actual project, students have the opportunity to see what I've done to capture my family's history by looking through my albums. After hearing students talk about the albums and answering questions about how they can get started, it's time to tell them about the project. I tell them that the albums they looked through are a "sneak peek" at a project they will be doing in the coming weeks. I then distribute several form letters for the students to fill in their individual information. We mail them to various agencies that may be able to facilitate the research. For example, one agency we write to is the Genealogical Society of Utah, 50 East North Temple Street, Salt Lake City, UT, 84150.

Another preplanning suggestion is to book your school's computer lab for several sessions of Internet research. If your computer lab is like ours, booking early is the only way you'll be assured of getting in there at a time that facilitates your project plans. You may find it helpful to purchase a copy, or several copies, of a book that deals with genealogy and ancestry as these books are great for "read-aloud" purposes and can serve as an important reference for the research.

Day one of our genealogy unit begins with a read-aloud featuring excerpts from the book by Lila Perl titled *The Great Ancestor Hunt.* While reading, I use "think-aloud" to clarify vocabulary and make connections. Once the spark that was initially seen during the anticipatory period has been rekindled, students are ready to begin. I distribute the project paper going over the requirements. In most academic workshops, the mini-lesson is a component. Therefore, the mini-lesson for day one covers how to write a bibliography correctly. Each day of the unit begins with an opening activity that includes reading in some fashion. Some days, the opening is a read-aloud, other days feature shared reading, while others may be an independent reading or journaling activity. The mini-lessons include topics like how to "surf the Net" effectively, read a family tree, make time lines, and create scrapbooks.

Not only are my students engaged in the activities for this unit, but parental involvement increases as well. I've had parents come to me years later and give their thanks for including a real-world project and for allowing them to be able to really help their child with a project that deals with a familiar topic. Far too often, parents are frustrated when they cannot help their children with homework and projects. "Who in the World Are You?" gives parents the chance to get involved with their child's learning because they feel confident and comfortable that they can help.

I'm sure you'll agree that the benefits of this type of project are plentiful. The project can be adapted to fit almost any grade level and fits nicely into both language arts and social studies curriculums. "Who in the World Are You?" enables the teacher to address a number of standards with one unit. Furthermore, cross-curricular links are easily made, and students can see the relevancy of reading, writing, and research to their own lives.

Helpful Tips

- Generate a form letter to send to various genealogy agencies.
- Book your school's computer lab a few weeks ahead of beginning the unit.
- Try writing grants to help pay for the scrapbooking supplies, or contact local craft shops to see if they will donate some supplies.
- Share your own albums or those of others, to help spark your students' creativity.

CHAPTER 28

Using Self-Publishing as a Gateway for Critical Reading

Stuart Albright

Durham, North Carolina

S tudents feel invested in the process of reading when they understand the importance of carefully crafted prose. In my high school
classes, students often make their greatest leaps as readers when they
struggle through the task of creating their own short stories. By reading
and critiquing each other's work, they begin to see the value of character development, exposition, plot, and description.

Connecting Reading and Writing

I decided early on as a teacher that creative writing would become an
essential component to my classes. Many of my students showed

tremendous apathy toward reading. They did not see why reading mattered. It was simply a hoop to cross. But as they began to write their own stories, sharing the pain and the joy and the unique perspective that they each brought to my room, they quickly realized how important it would be to read literature that modeled the best practices of story-telling. The final breakthrough for this process came when I first stumbled upon the surprisingly simple process of self-publishing my students' work.

▨ Students as Authors

In the fall of 2005, I created a publishing company called McKinnon Press, with the goal of producing student work from some of my creative writing and English classes. I had just released my own self-published memoir, *Blessed Returns,* which provided me with some valuable insights into the world of book publication and distribution. Creative writing had never been offered at my school until then, and I started out with one class of 30 students each semester. The following year, more than 150 students signed up to take my creative writing classes. The increase can be attributed to McKinnon Press.

Each one of my creative writing classes produces a professional-quality anthology of their best work. The books are available online through my company's Web site, www.mckinnonpress.com. The Web site is full of information about the books and the authors behind each book. To date, McKinnon Press has published the writings of 246 authors from my high school in eight anthologies, plus two novels from students and two individual collections of short stories. The books are a great way to get students motivated about learning. When my students see the final product, they are absolutely thrilled. Their families are delighted as well. Parents pass out copies to all their neighbors and coworkers, proudly announcing the new "author in the family." I have seen students with limited writing abilities and almost no self-confidence absolutely flourish in this environment.

A glance at any one of the anthologies reveals a tremendous amount of diversity. My students come from all races, ethnicities, socioeconomic backgrounds, and cliques from within our school. I work hard to create a family atmosphere in each class. This is absolutely essential when you are asking students to take intellectual risks and to write about subjects that matter to them personally.

My students see McKinnon Press as more than just a way to get their names in print. It is also an avenue to help them develop into better writers. I regularly hear from former students now in college who say that creative writing has helped them dramatically improve their essay writing, as well as their analytical thinking as a whole. They miss our class's openness to new ideas, and they actually long for the discipline of writing and reading every day. These conversations convince me that McKinnon Press is making an impact.

Authors as Readers

The "student as author" concept can work on a much smaller scale. When students create their own prose, they begin to feel more ownership over their development as critical thinkers. Students learn that if they want to become a better writer—while telling a story that has meaning in their own life—they must first develop a consistent habit of reading various genres, diverse topics, and unique styles of writing that may be different from their own.

Students in my classes who once hated reading are now pestering me for books to read that could open their eyes to new ways of writing. They do this constantly, loudly, and incessantly. It's a beautiful thing.

Teachers as Innovators of Reading and Writing

I firmly believe that the basic concept behind McKinnon Press can be replicated at other schools. Several English teachers at neighboring high schools have already asked me to help them set up a similar program in their own classes. As I collaborate with teachers locally and across the state, my own enthusiasm for this project continues to grow. I love the challenge of bringing professionals from all walks of life to the table. As I teach them, I get new ideas in return. It is a collaborative process that informs me as much as it informs them.

Now that I have a body of professional-looking stories from several years' worth of classes, I use these anthologies as models for incoming classes of apathetic readers and writers. When students critique a prose selection that was written by a classmate, they bring a level of gravity and interest that is rarely seen in a high school classroom. They slip into metacognitive thinking about reading and writing without batting an eye. The whole process has brought me closer to my students than I ever thought possible.

Helpful Tips

- Check out www.lulu.com for more information about self-publishing. Lulu is the company I use as a distributor for my students' work. They have very low overhead costs, and they make it easy to learn the whole process. Other companies such as iUniverse offer similar programs.
- Also check out my publishing site, www.mckinnonpress.com, for ideas about publishing anthologies and novels of student writing.

CHAPTER **29**

Score a BINGO
in Reading

Mikki Nuckols

Idaho Falls, Idaho

E very year I hear the same thing from my students: "I don't have
time to read (with sports, scouts, or music)." "There's nothing good
to read in the library." "Those books are stupid." For years, boys have
tended to struggle with reading for pleasure. Girls—who seem to lean
toward the language arts (leaving science and math behind)—have little
or no trouble finding a good book to read. Being the mother of both a
girl reader and a boy nonreader, this became a concern at home.

When I started teaching ten years ago, Accelerated Reading (AR)
was just making a debut in our state. I jumped on the bandwagon
hoping that this would get my nonreading students motivated to read or
at least want to read for pleasure. I had some success the first couple of
years, but then started seeing the trend of nonreaders (both genders)
creep back into my class. Many of the students totally stopped reading
if they weren't going to make their goals. AR suggested some type of
reward for making each quarterly reading goal. To continue to motivate
the students, the rewards each time had to get bigger and better. I was

going broke just trying to get my kids to read, as our school did not have the money to fund the reward part of the program. I even had one teacher tell me that the program was stupid. She said, "Kids should just want to read." I wish that were true. I found that after students had used the AR program for six school years, the students were getting burnt out on the whole testing process. I also found that if there wasn't a test for the book, or the reading level didn't fall into the students' assigned reading level, good books weren't getting read.

Three years ago, I attended a class on differentiated instructional practices. While I was there, the instructors were giving ideas on how to get the kids motivated to write. They suggested a BINGO sheet. Each square had a different writing idea (e.g., a letter to a pen pal, a narrative essay, or a speech). I took this concept and adapted it to the different genres in reading (one genre per square). I revised this BINGO sheet to fit the age groups and interests of my students. Each of the BINGO sheets has the same genres, just scrambled so that there are twenty-five different sheets. On the first day of school, I pass out the sheets in random order so that only one or two students end up with the same sheet per class. The students don't get to choose which sheets they are assigned.

The instructions for this assignment are simple: students are to read five books in a BINGO (up/down, side-to-side, or diagonal) during a nine-week period. Each square on the BINGO sheet represents a different genre (e.g., fantasy, horror/fright, biography). The books must be 150 pages for fiction and 100 pages for nonfiction (minimum). I have found that for some of my low readers, I need to make page allowances, but for the most part, the students usually read much larger books. I also count some books as multiple books depending on the number of pages and the amount of time it took to read the book. If my students read *Harry Potter and the Deathly Hallows* in one week, that counts as only one book. If it took them more than a month, I usually count it as two.

During my first year of teaching, I had remedial eighth-grade language arts students. The "Poetry" square was nothing that any of them really wanted to venture out to read. The "Parent Pick" square had parents recommending books that we did not carry in our school library. As a result, I changed both of these squares to a more "student enjoyable" genre. This year I have 125 students in my five classes, with only 2 students not reading the required ten books (two BINGOs) before the end of the semester—and these two students each read nine books.

I have teachers ask me about accountability. I can say that I'm sure that some students have not read the entire book; I have them talk to me before I write the book on their BINGO sheet. The students give me a summary of the story. If I have not read the book, I quickly scan areas of the story to brief myself on the plot. If I am satisfied that they did read the book, I give them credit on the BINGO sheet. I maintain all BINGO sheets during the course of the term. I don't let them fill in the squares for the book. At the end of the term, the students are graded on their BINGO sheet (I usually give 5 points per book). The hardest part of the entire BINGO project is that when a student finally finds the author or genre that makes them truly enjoy reading, they still have to go off-topic to read the other "squares."

In addition to the BINGO sheets, I also do one project a term (over one book from their BINGO sheet) to make sure that they pay attention to details. This project is the final grade of the term and is worth 50 points. However, it is not the "final" for my class.

This project is based on any book the student chooses from the present term's BINGO and ranges from creating a music CD cover, creating a game board, writing a letter to the author, writing a new ending to a book, or submitting a book fair display. The CD requires the student to draw a picture of anything from the story that hasn't already been illustrated (such as the cover of the book). On the back of the page, they write a poem or song summarizing the story. For the board game project, they create a game using either the plot or setting and characters from their books. They may write letters to any of the living authors asking questions about writing or the story itself. If they want a different ending to the final chapter, they can rewrite the last chapter. My favorite project is the "science fair" approach. The students list title, characters, setting, plot, conflict, theme, mood, and a brief summary of the story for one book they have read during the term. They display it on the "book fair" three-fold poster board for their fellow classmates to judge.

Best practices in teaching suggest that students should have some say in their learning. With this variety of different projects, students can choose the project that best fits either their likes for a project or the novel for the specific genre. Over the past eighteen weeks, I'm finding that more nonreaders are now reading, and there is much less complaining about "no good books to read."

Book BINGO Menu

Name: _____

(Books must equal a minimum of 100 pages nonfiction and 150 pages fiction)

Fairy Tales/ Folktales	Biography	Fright/Horror	Animal Story	Summer Book
Humor	Reader's Choice Awards	Adventure	Historical Fiction	Movie Title
Cultures	Science Fiction (text)	Your Choice	Mystery	War Story (text)
Number in Title (text)	Comics/Riddles	Copyright before 1950	Series Book	Ancient History
Newberry Award	Mythology	Teen-age Story	Sports	Fantasy

CHAPTER 30

Short-Cycle Assessment in a Reading Workshop

A Collaboration Between Teacher and Student

Darrell Yater

Cincinatti, Ohio

Designing the Assessment

Assessment has been an ongoing and frustrating journey for me over the years. I have used reading inventories, but with over a hundred seventh graders, I can't use this on every child. My district began using a computer-based reading inventory, but the single score for each student didn't provide enough information. Using gradebook categories like homework, tests, and quizzes didn't help me understand strengths and weaknesses, so I switched to a standards-based grading and reporting system. I felt this was a step in the right direction, but I was waiting weeks or even the whole quarter to get enough data to analyze.

I have tried, revised, and revamped assessment approaches in my classroom more times than I care to count. My goal has never changed: to get an accurate picture of my students' abilities that would allow me to guide them instructionally so that they leave my classroom a better reader than when they entered it. My approach has taken many roads, some rockier than others. Now, through the use of short-cycle standards-based assessments, I have begun traveling a smoother road with a more seamless integration of data-driven decisions informing the instruction and grouping of students in my class.

Short-cycle assessments are given more frequently to get a quick measure of student ability. These assessments are given about every three weeks and are based on the state standards. As the name implies, they are short, both in length as well as in duration between administering them. The way they are structured, the answer document provides real-time data aligned to standards. This allows for more immediate intervention with students who are in need of more support. As I have found, it is crucial that I, as the teacher, be able to access the information quickly so that it is used in a timely fashion.

What may be equally important to my accessing the information is the understanding and accessibility of data to the students. Providing a format by which students are able to understand the information and its implications for their success is essential. They are able to analyze and interpret their own strengths and weaknesses. Bringing them into the equation, letting them understand what the scores mean as well as how and why I use them, has empowered them to take ownership and responsibility for their understanding of the concepts.

▧ Planning

As I plan my quarter, I begin by grouping the objectives into logical chunks. My district provides a curriculum calendar with all objectives grouped into the quarter in which they are meant to be taught. Within the quarter, I have the autonomy to decide the order in which to teach them, how many units to develop, and the resources to use in order to meet the benchmarks. I look for objectives that I feel I can reasonably link together and address within one unit. I always try to link the type of writing to the reading goals as well.

I believed that if I could address these goals in a mostly narrative unit, I would be able to model through a common text, have students apply it in their self-selected reading, and supplement with nonfiction related to the topic of the common text.

For example:

Reading Process 5. Use organizational strategies (e.g., rough outlines, diagrams, maps, webs, and Venn diagrams).

Reading Process 9. Independently read books for various purposes (e.g., for enjoyment, for literary experience, to gain information or to perform a task).

Reading Application—Literary 2. Analyze the features of the setting and their importance in a text.

Reading Application—Literary 3. Identify the main and minor events of the plot, and explain how each incident gives rise to the next.

Reading Application—Informational 1. Use text features, such as chapter titles, headings, and subheadings; parts of books including the index, appendix, and table of contents; and online tools (search engines) to locate information (maps, webs, and Venn diagrams) to plan writing.

▨ Assessment Creation

Before I create the assessment, I analyze the state assessment. First, I analyze the questions from the assessment to align my understanding and expectation of that goal. Then I choose an excerpt of text to use and create ten to fifteen questions based on the objectives stated in the unit. Each question is aligned to an objective from the state standards and mirrors the format.

For example:

Read pages 62–67 in *The Outsiders* and answer the following questions:

Reading Process Standard

6. Which statement helps create a visual image for the reader?
   A. I climbed over the barbed-wire fence without saying anything else.
   B. It was a small church, real old and spooky and spiderwebby.
   C. It was only last night that Dally and I had sat down behind those girls at the Nightly Double.
   D. I was hardly awake when Johnny and I leaped off the train into a meadow.

Reading Application—Information

7. Since Ponyboy and Johnny are hiding out in a rural community, if you wanted to look up information on farms, what would be the best resource to use?
   A. Continue reading *The Outsiders*.
   B. Use an encyclopedia and look up the word *farm*.
   C. Look up *farm* in a thesaurus.
   D. Use the Internet to Google "the outsiders."

Reading Application—Literary

9. What does Ponyboy mean by the following statement on page 65? "There are things worse than being a greaser."
   A. He doesn't want to be a greaser anymore.
   B. He realizes that some people have harder lives than greasers.
   C. He thinks he'd rather be a farmer now.
   D. Being a soc is worse than a greaser.

The answer document allows for much student input. They rate their level of confidence as they answer the questions by placing a check mark in one of the first two columns. Their answer is listed in the third column. To grade them, I put a 1 in the standard column if the answer is correct and an X if it is incorrect. I can easily tally each standard column to get a raw score. Then students analyze why they missed a question by reviewing the correct answer and determining whether it was a simple mistake or something in which they need more instruction. The data are then analyzed by the teacher and the student to determine areas where additional support or enrichment is needed. This analysis can be as simple as using the raw score or by adjusting the score and using the areas where students determine themselves to need more instruction. At the beginning of the year, I use the raw scores, but as the year goes on, students become more proficient at self-analysis.

For example:

Question	Confident	Unsure	Answer	RP	RAL	RAI	Simple Mistake	Further Study
1	✔		A			1		
2		✔	C			X	✔	
3	✔		B			1		
4	✔		D			1		
5		✔	A	X				✔
6		✔	C	X				✔
7	✔		A			X	✔	
8	✔		D	1				
9	✔		B		1			
10	✔		B	1				
11		✔	A	X				✔
12	✔		D	X				
13	✔		A	1				
Short Answer	✔				2			
Scores				2/4	4/6	3/5		

⬚ What to Do With the Data

I have heard a resounding "HELP" echo through the school halls when teachers are asked to analyze and use data. I know that teachers innately want to help students but sometimes may lack the tools to translate all the data into a practical and feasible implementation plan.

Before the data can be shared, students must be informed about the objectives from the state. I share with my students the different standards from the state department of education and explain in student-friendly terms the meaning of each. In Ohio, one of the standards is reading process. I communicate that this is their ability to adjust their rate and purpose for reading and utilize strategies like self-monitoring, questioning, and activating prior knowledge. During class, I will let them know if an assignment or activity directly links to this standard. This may be as simple as verbally reminding them, posting on the wall a sign about what we will learn in the lesson, or putting a label on the top of an assignment.

In this manner, when it comes time to have students self-assess their short-cycle assessment results, they understand the areas listed and what those standards mean. Students are able to determine which standard they feel is their weakness. They are able to keep track of this on a data sheet in their portfolio.

Data collected from the short-cycle assessment must be able to be used in a timely fashion. Therefore, after scoring the assessment, I revise seating charts. This may seem unrelated, but in order to effectively and quickly get to the students, I need to have accurate groupings. These are designated based on the assessment data so that all reading process students are sitting in small groups together, all students scoring low in literary reading application are grouped together, and so on. Students are aware of how and why the seating arrangement is formed. It may be obvious, but students are not in rows. Seats are arranged in groups of four to six at a table. In this manner, all students can focus on one area for direct instruction or may be focused on their group if small-group instruction is needed. Their understanding of this is important in their ability to see the value in the instruction and the relevance to themselves. When small groups have different assignments or when I meet with one group and do a different activity than with a previous group, students understand it is because I am differentiating based on the standard where they need the most support.

An important distinction that needs to be made here is the concept of flexible grouping. Students are not relegated to a seat and left there permanently, nor are students identified with a weakness and permanently labeled as such. Students are grouped based on need and on data. These needs may change as the year progresses based on the content covered. Early on, a student may be identified as needing to develop their literary analysis because they struggle with understanding the importance of setting and inferring theme. Later in the year, the priority may shift to informational reading applications in the area of understanding structure and features of informational text. This student does not stay in a group focused on literary analysis all year. He or she is regrouped with each assessment so that the instruction is timely and addresses the individual needs of the student.

I believe time is of the essence in the classroom. The flexible grouping allows for small-group instruction, which maximizes the instructional time. The revised seating chart based on assessment data means the groups are mostly formed. I am able to give instructions and begin to work with a small group while the other students are working more independently. Therefore, kids spend less time moving around the room trying to find their group assignment or work location for the day.

▨ Reading Workshop

I needed a structure that would be most flexible with grouping students and allow for the most individualized instruction. I knew class novels and whole-group instruction weren't getting to all the students' needs. The most effective structure I have found is the reading workshop approach.

Small groups, or invitational groups, in which some students are put in a group and other students are invited to join if they would like to participate, are where a lot of the focused instruction takes place. These groups allow me to focus on specific reading strategies identified by the short-cycle assessment such as activating prior knowledge, visualization techniques, questioning text, self-monitoring tools, and so on in a guided manner. While I meet with this group, I usually use a short piece of text I have chosen to illustrate the strategy or remediate a skill noted from the short-cycle assessment while the rest of the class applies that concept to more independently selected reading material. Other students may also be rotating through other activities such as word sorts, WebQuests, literature circle meetings, and so on. The key elements are that the group is based on need, taught in a guided manner, and the other students are engaged in other authentic activities.

When I find areas of weakness, I utilize think-alouds frequently to model the type of textual interaction and analysis required. At this point, I own the thinking and allow the students to view my interaction and analysis. In guided groups, I can begin to share the thinking with the students, inviting them to be active participants through questioning and especially through the use of graphic organizers. As their comfort level and competency level increase, I can back farther out of the picture by just offering support and guidance until they own the skill or strategy and are able to articulate it to others. During the small-group instruction, I am still in the guidance phase. However, my goal is to help move them to higher levels of independence.

Assessment is a powerful tool in my classroom and informs the instruction. I always begin by identifying the key objectives to be covered in a unit, build the essential understandings and questions from there, and then think about the types of assessments that are appropriate. Obviously, short-cycle assessments are part of that, but also included are assessments based on multiple intelligences, formal and informal assessments, and summative and formative assessments. A bank of instructional activities is also created. This is where flexibility is so important. Based on assessment data, I may use some activities, not use others, or create new ones. A variety of whole-group and small-group instruction as well as flexible groupings of students allows me to respond to the data as frequently as possible.

As you can see, the short-cycle assessment is a piece of the puzzle, but intricately connected to so many other pieces. When this is put in place with all the other elements, the picture of student success becomes clear. I share this puzzle with my students, listen to them, and allow them to have a true understanding of how and why things happen in the classroom. The road to data-driven instruction has been much smoother with this approach. I feel like my students and I get farther down the road and arrive there faster than with any other system I have used.

Helpful Tips

- Create short-cycle assessments linked to specific objectives.
- Analyze the data and use them in a timely manner.
- Involve the students in the analysis of their own data.
- Create seating charts based on students of similar instructional needs based on data.
- Flexibly group students often.
- Provide small-group instruction to students based on short-cycle assessment data.
- Create instructional activities for all students based on assessment data.

Index

**CORWIN
PRESS**

The Corwin Press logo—a raven striding across an open book—represents the union of courage and learning. Corwin Press is committed to improving education for all learners by publishing books and other professional development resources for those serving the field of PreK–12 education. By providing practical, hands-on materials, Corwin Press continues to carry out the promise of its motto: **"Helping Educators Do Their Work Better."**